Who Killed Canadian History?

Who Killed Canadian History?

J. L. GRANATSTEIN

HarperPerennial
HarperCollins*Publishers*Ltd
A Phyllis Bruce Book

For Robert Ivan Martin,
old friend and stout colleague

http://www.harpercanada.com

Jacket photo credits (clockwise from top left):
Louis Riel (c 1876) — Provincial Archives of Manitoba (N5730)
Pierre Elliott Trudeau (just before being elected leader of the Liberal Party on
April 7, 1968) — CANAPRESS Photo Service (Chuck Mitchell)
Nellie McClung (one of the Famous Five, a group of Canadian women who peti-
tioned in 1929 to amend the BNA Act to allow the word "persons"
to apply to women as well as men) — CANAPRESS Photo Service
Sir John A. Macdonald — National Archives of Canada (C-6513)
René Lévesque (following the victory of the Parti Québécois over the Liberal Party in
the provincial election on November 15, 1976) — CANAPRESS Photo Service
The Fathers of Confederation (at the Charlottetown Conference, September 1864)
— National Archives of Canada (PAC/AP C-733)
Canadian troops (arriving over the bridge at Beachhead) — National Archives of
Canada/Canadian Department of National Defence Collection (PA-132850)

First published in hardcover by HarperCollins: 1998
First HarperPerennial edition: 1999

Canadian Cataloguing in Publication Data

Granatstein, J. L., 1939-
Who killed Canadian history?

"A Phyllis Bruce book."
Includes index.
ISBN 0-00-255759-2 (bound)
ISBN 0-00-638607-5 (pbk)

1. Canada - History - Study and Teaching - Government policy.   2. Multiculturalism -
Canada.   3. Education and state - Canada.   I. Title.

LA417.5.G73 1998   379.71   C97-932321-5

---

99 00 01 02 03   HC   10 9 8 7 6 5 4 3 2 1

Contents

Acknowledgements

I am most grateful to Milena Ivkovic for splendid research assistance. An excellent young historian in her own right, she is also a new teacher and has collected vast amounts of material for me, organized it carefully, commented on it astutely, and helped me greatly. She is, of course, in no way responsible for the judgments I have made.

I have also been assisted by a number of teachers who took the time to talk to me, by former university colleagues, and by friends William Kaplan, Bill Young, Graham Rawlinson, Catherine Salo, and Daniel Robinson (who provided the Bad Writing Contest winners' announcement and other materials). Bill Blaikie, MP, obtained the Manitoba legislature debates on the teaching of Canadian history for me. Rudyard Griffiths and the new Dominion Institute let me use its Angus Reid Group polling results on Canadian youths' historical knowledge, and Dan Gardner, late of the Ontario Ministry of Education and now of the *Ottawa Citizen*, gave assistance with curricular and other sources. My graduate school classmate John Gates, now of the College of Wooster, helped with some United States comparisons, and Sondra Schmidt briefed me on the superb scholarship system in Germany. Rosemary Shipton edited this manuscript, as she has so many others for me, with great skill. I am grateful to them all.

J. L. G.

Summer 1997

Preface to the Second Edition

Whose history would we teach? That is the usual response from education ministers and school board officials to questions why so little history is taught in our schools. It suggests that for a linguistically and geographically divided nation, for a country populated by immigrants, there are many histories—far too many for us to teach. Better to offer none at all. But the answer should be that we will teach the history of Canada, of all its people, of their role in developing this nation, and of Canada's place in the world. Somehow, unfortunately, that all-too-reasonable response never stirs to action those who shape education policies. Yet the question is answered every day in our classrooms in ways that might surprise parents and taxpayers.

Brad is a bright eight year old, a reader, a talker, and a budding violinist. George and Suzanne, his parents and my friends, pay $8000 a year to send him to a small private school near their home in the Maritimes because, they are convinced, it offers good teaching and quality learning. In his "enhanced" grade 2 class this last school year, Brad began to be taught something about his country, and he learned about Canadian geography, Quebec sugar bushes, and the Group of Seven. He also wrote five brief historical reports. The first was on Samuel de Champlain, with substantial emphasis on the tribulations his child-bride suffered. The second report examined the extinction of the Beothuk, thanks to shootings, disease, and starvation caused by the white men. The third report was about Louis Riel, whom Brad called a Métis hero but who was labelled a traitor in his day because he stood up for his people. The next report outlined the opposition and frustration endured by Canada's first female doctor, Emily Jennings Stowe, as she sought to practise. The last, on the maltreatment of Japanese Canadians during the Second World War, dealt with what happened to people when, as Brad wrote, the government decided it could not trust anyone who looked Japanese.

Brad's papers are impressive for a child his age, but profoundly depressing in what they suggest goes on today in our schools. The first exposure to the history of Canada that Brad received in class combined seemingly unrelated events and individuals— without much regard for chronology—that were judged important by his teacher. Though provincial guidelines offer little direction for early primary grades, the teacher was reflecting what she deemed to be the province's educational priorities. The material taught stressed the existence of anti-Aboriginal, anti-Métis, and anti-Asian racism, as well as male sexism and discrimination against women, as if these issues were and always had been the primary identifying characteristics of Canada. Riel, the first "hero" to whom Brad was exposed, in a country that always bewails its lack of them, was a man who, after a kangaroo court trial, ordered the murder of a loud-mouthed Ontario Orangeman and, to boot, was a crazed religious fanatic who led two armed rebellions. Riel might be a hero and a leader to the Métis, but he has no credentials as a hero to all Canadians, and no school should teach his life that way.

Indeed, since all education is about choices, we might ask why Brad should learn about Riel rather than Sir John A. Macdonald, someone whose accomplishments were more important and much longer lasting. Or about Emily Stowe rather than Frederick Banting, the discoverer of insulin. Or about the maltreatment of Japanese Canadians rather than the successful integration of millions of immigrants.

The reasons, unfortunately, are all too obvious, and they provide the real answer to the question, Whose history should we teach? The choices being made every day in Brad's school are political, not historical. They aim to teach a lesson about racism and sexism, not history. The history taught is that of the grievers among us, the present-day crusaders against public policy or discrimination. The history omitted is that of the Canadian nation and people.

There was racism and sexism in Canada's past, just as there is today. These are not the only themes in our history, however, though one would be hard-pressed to prove it from the history education offered to Canada's young schoolchildren. Sadly, Brad's experience is echoed in classrooms from Newfoundland to British Columbia. What are we saying to our sons and daughters? What are we doing to our history? Somewhere, somehow, we have completely lost our way.

Canada must be one of the few nations in the world, certainly one of the few Western industrialized states, that does not make an effort to teach its history positively and thoroughly to its young people. It must be one of the few political entities to overlook its own cultural traditions—the European civilization on which our nation is founded—on the grounds that they would systematically discriminate against those who come from other cultures. The effects of these policies on a generation of students are all around us as the twentieth century draws to a close.

History is important, I believe, because it is the way a nation, a people, and an individual learn who they are, where they came from, and how and why their world has turned out as it has. We do not simply exist in a contemporary world. We have a past, if only we would try to grapple with it. History teaches us a sense of change over time. History is memory, inspiration, and commonality—and a nation without memory is every bit as adrift as an amnesiac wandering the streets. History matters, and we forget this truth at our peril.

It is now a year since this book appeared. It has been quoted in Parliament and in provincial legislatures and reviewed more extensively in the media than most books of this kind. It has generated hundreds of letters to me from teachers, parents, and grandparents, alarmed at what is going on—or not going on—in our schools. The title has become a catchphrase, one that can be dropped into unrelated articles or everyday speech without any necessity to explain its origin. And to my delight and total astonishment, it has sold well above 10,000 copies in hardcover to date and, as this paper edition suggests, the volume will likely continue to remain in bookstores for some time to come.

Most rewarding of all, there are some signs that the message of this little book is beginning to be accepted. The Manitoba government has abandoned its plan to drop Canadian history from the high school curriculum. The Ontario government has introduced a public school curriculum that offers youngsters substantially more Canadian history, though it has yet to do anything significant for high school students. In Alberta, the Edmonton public schools joined forces with the University of Alberta History Department to re-design the history curriculum for grades 7, 8, and 9, and is in the process of expanding its reach into grades 10 and 11. The Edmonton schools are also creating a two course series on "The Military History of Canada" that, while aimed at one secondary school, the Vimy

Ridge Academy, is receiving substantial interest from other high schools. This is real progress and other provinces are soon going to be forced to meet a growing public demand for more Canadian history.

At the same time, the private and public sectors are becoming interested in our history anew. Red Wilson, the Chair of the powerful telecommunications firm BCE, has called for the creation of a "Foundation for the History of Canada" and has offered $500,000 of his own funds to get it started. He has attracted substantial interest from his business peers. The National Film Board has allocated $1 million a year for five years to create a World Wide Web site devoted to Canadian history, and the Canadian Broadcasting Corporation is spending millions to produce a lavishly produced multi-hour television history of Canada. No one knows what will emerge from these ventures as yet, either in terms of quality or the interpretation of the past that will be adopted, but the activity is all but unprecedented—and heartening.

I myself have seen this growing interest in our past at the Canadian War Museum in Ottawa where I became the Director and CEO on July 1, 1998. The War Museum is well over a century old, and it has long been the orphan child of the Canadian national museum system. Underfunded, its exhibits static, its buildings completely inadequate, the War Museum had watched its attendance dwindle, and many harboured the secret fear that the government was simply waiting for the last veterans to disappear so a museum that celebrated outdated virtues could be closed down.

It was not because the CWM lacked extraordinary material that it seemed irrelevant. First, it holds the wonderful official war art collection created during the First and Second World Wars, the Korean War, and a succession of peacekeeping and peacemaking missions. In all, there are 12,500 pieces of art, a larger collection of Canadian art than that held by the National Gallery of Canada. It contains large samplings of work by the best Canadian artists, including members of the Group of Seven—to see Franz Johnston's superb paintings of Great War flying training, for example, is to stand in awe—Alex Colville, Paraskeva Clark, and Molly Lamb Bobak. The CWM has one of the world's great collections of military vehicles and a huge uniform collection including the coatee General Brock was wearing when he was killed in action during the War of 1812. It holds a huge array of Canadian-won Victoria Crosses, a massive small arms collection, the best military history library in Canada, and an archives with upwards of 500 manuscript collections.

No one knows of this superb collection. The art has scarcely been seen—conditions in the War Museum on Sussex Drive in Ottawa, the former Public Archives of Canada building built early in the twentieth century, are so inadequate that art works on paper can be displayed only for limited periods. The Museum premises are so small that only one percent of the collection can be shown, and the warehouse—a former Ottawa streetcar barn—is far from ideal as a repository or a venue for visitors. Moreover, the archives is almost unuseable because the funds to organize it so that researchers could plumb its treasures have never been available.

But matters are changing. The Donner Canadian Foundation has made a very large grant to the Museum to send a travelling exhibit of the best war art around the country and to produce a coffee-table book on the collection. At last, Canadians will be able to see some of their hidden treasures. The archives is being sorted and catalogued. And best of all, the Government of Canada in November 1998 gave the War Museum some twenty acres of land on the soon-to-be disposed-of Canadian Forces Base Rockcliffe as the site for a new purpose-built museum. All this has been urged along by a media which has begun to focus on the need to recognize Canada's military past in an appropriate way. There is still a long march ahead before a new War Museum is open to the public, but the first steps have surely been taken.

None of this would have happened ten or twenty years ago. The media would have paid no attention to a book entitled *Who Killed Canadian History?* The provinces would have continued their shameful pandering to every trendy fashion and slashed away at content-oriented courses on Canadian history. Business and the media would have expressed not a jot or a tittle of interest in the past. The treasures in the War Museum would have been allowed to molder away.

But today, something is happening out there. Canadians feel a growing concern that the nation is in danger of fragmentation, and not only from Quebec separatism. There are fears that free trade, globalization, and the overpowering force of American culture are gravely weakening the ties that bind the nation. If Canada is to survive, we must know what the nation was, is, and will be. Without a past that we know and share, we can only be like lost children wandering despondently in a trackless wilderness. At the Canadian War Museum, as the veterans of the Second World War and Korea inexorably age, I see every day the desire to ensure that their legacy is passed on. To them, to me, that legacy is one of courage and selflessness and, without that legacy, freedom would have perished from the earth. That history matters to us all, and at last we seem to be agreeing that it does.

I claim no credit for this happy tendency for it is clear that *Who Killed Canadian History?* simply caught a wave that was already building. What is important now is to ensure that the pressure is kept up, that parents demand history be included in the curriculum, that schools stretch their existing curricula to the fullest to include the past in their offerings, and that the media, business, and governments continue to speed the process.

We do have a history. Canadians have an honourable past that merits study and that can unite us all, native born and recent immigrants. We have a country to build. We have a nation to save.

Toronto and Ottawa,
March 1999

CHAPTER 1

What History?
Which History?

C onservatives falsify the past, socialists falsify the future, and liberals falsify the present, so someone once said. It may even be true—in most countries. Canada is different.

Ours is a nation where everyone—liberal, socialist, and conservative—seems to be engaged in an unthinking conspiracy to eliminate Canada's past. The public schools and high schools scarcely teach history, so busy are they fighting racism, teaching sex education, or instructing English as a second language for recent immigrants. Fewer and fewer university professors write history in anything but undigestible small chunks of interest only to specialists. The media use history only to search for villainy, if they use it at all, or else they mangle it beyond recognition to prove a contemporary argument. There are no heroes in our past to stir the soul, and no myths on which a national spirit can be built—or so we are told. The ordinary Canadian citizen, inundated by American media and Fourth-of-July rah-rah patriotism, scarcely knows that Canada has a past. Wasn't George Washington Canada's first prime minister? Didn't Davy Crockett settle the West?

Indeed, it sometimes seems that Canadians have deliberately deconstructed their past, sacrificing it for the good of a mythical present. The French Canadians were brave voyageurs who fought the Iroquois and the English, posing, in between, for Cornelius Krieghoff. The Loyalists were slaveholding Anglo-Saxon white males whose anti-democratic instincts were all too evident. Confederation was a scheme by railway investors to protect their profits. The Riel rebellions were attempts to thwart efforts to crush the idyllic civilizations of native peoples under the weight of technology and speculators. If Canada participated in the two world wars, it should not have, because Canadians are peace-keepers by nature. This ignorant bowdlerization, where it has any intention at all, serves a nation that today sees itself as bilingual, multicultural, pacifist, and committed to social justice.

These are not evil national goals, to be sure, though they scarcely represent the Canada that most Canadians know. Even though each generation always writes its own history, the past is not supposed to be twisted completely out of shape to serve present ends. To do so mocks the dead and makes fools of the living; it reduces the past to a mere perspective on the present; and it imprisons history in a cage of consciously constructed quasi-fabrications. As Germans, Japanese, and Russians surely know, nations have to overcome their histories. Canada, thank heavens, has a relatively benign history, but, where we consider it at all, we struggle against the past as if our forebears had committed atrocities and innumerable evils, and regularly practised genocidal behaviour. The task of the current generation is to build on the past, to understand it, and, where necessary, to triumph over it. If we cannot, the fault is not in what happened one, two, or three centuries ago, but in ourselves.

History is important because it helps people know themselves. It tells them who they were and who they are; it is the collective memory of humanity that situates them in their time and place; and it provides newcomers with some understanding of the society in which they have chosen to live. Of course, the collective memory undergoes constant revision, restructuring, and rewriting, but whatever its form it reveals anew to each generation a common fund of knowledge, traditions, values, and ideas that help to explain our existence and the mistakes and successes of the past.

Surely this process is all the more important in a world that is shrinking technologically and, simultaneously, fragmenting into ethnic and national groupings. Canada is part of a global economy and an integrated North American trade group, both of which bring stress to citizens and to governments. It is a nation of regions, languages, religions, and disparate classes and cultures. There is much to disunify Canadians and, all too often, very little to join them together. History is one such unifying factor: the way of life and the traditions that men and women created in this nation. For incomprehensible reasons, we have not passed this knowledge on to our children and to those who have recently arrived in Canada.

This neglect is foolhardy, for the past has shaped us all. Canada was a French colony, then a British colony, and now, many might argue, an American one. This colonization has stunted Canadians' psychological development in important ways. Robert MacNeil, the Canadian-born newscaster who made PBS news a nightly event, wrote of his childhood: "One of the psychologically crippling things, part of the colonial wound that never healed at least in the psyches of my generation, was that we grew up reading books that were all written and published about people who lived . . . in other countries. We were not a written-about people. If you are not a written-about people, if you're not a storied people, you're not a people, you have no identity really." The fact is not that Canada has no past, but simply that its history has not been turned into story for Canadians. Much more Canadian history is written today than when MacNeil was a boy in Halifax, but it is as little understood by Canadians now as then.

Canadians have not tried to understand their past, so it should come as no surprise that they know little about it. Survey after survey has proven this ignorance beyond dispute. The Committee for an Independent Canada in 1974 sponsored a Canadian history test in some British Columbia schools and found that three-quarters of the participants could not name the premier of Quebec or the capital of New Brunswick, six in ten were unable to name a single Canadian author, and large numbers did not know what the British North America Act was. The next year, publisher Mel Hurtig conducted a national test that produced similar results. Two in three students could not name three prime ministers since the Second World War, or which Canadian had won the Nobel Peace Prize in 1957. Lack of knowledge of geography, history, and literature was staggering, and 62 percent of the students taking the test failed abysmally.

In his memoirs, *At Twilight in the Country*, Hurtig detailed the extraordinary response to the publication of the results. Parliamentarians and provincial leaders were outraged, newspapers wrote editorials lamenting the situation, and individuals and groups demanded that school curricula in Canada be changed to correct the situation. Predictably, nothing happened.

The Task Force on National Unity, led by Keith Spicer at the beginning of the 1990s, heard from countless Canadians that they did not know their history and that they wanted more of it taught in school. Spicer concluded: "We do not know enough about ourselves. Without a radically fresh approach to improving what we know about each other, our lack of knowledge of the basic realities of this country will continue to cripple efforts at accommodation." Again, nothing.

Then, in 1991, a national heritage test was conducted by the Association for Canadian Studies. Not surprisingly, the test again uncovered clear cultural gaps—English Canadians knew less Quebec history than Québécois did, and vice versa. The survey also found that Canadians, both French- and English-speaking, wanted more history and heritage taught in the schools and that they were concerned about how little they knew. Contrary to the popular myth, though, this was not because Canadian history was boring. Teach more history, the message went, and this common understanding might help tie Canadians together. Once more, no action resulted.

When Joanne Harris Burgess, a Canadian Studies professor at York University's Glendon College in Toronto, tested students in her course in 1997, she concluded: "I have noticed surprising, constantly growing gaps in my first-year students' knowledge of Canada." The results were startlingly similar to those Hurtig had found: two-thirds could not name a Canadian author; a large majority were unable to name the nation's first English- and French-speaking prime ministers; and more than half were unable to give the date of Confederation. "When the average mark of bright, interested Ontario high school graduates on this question-naire is 32.5 percent," Professor Burgess wrote, "it is not the students but Canadian history courses in our high schools that have failed. And that is a failure we as a nation cannot afford."

Similarly depressing results were found in a survey of young French- and English-speaking Canadians between the ages of eighteen and twenty-four conducted in late May 1997 by the Angus Reid Group for the Dominion Institute. Just 54 percent of respondents in the survey could identify John A. Macdonald as the nation's first prime minister, 33 percent were aware that Remembrance Day commemorated the end of the First World War, 35 percent knew what D-Day signified, 10 percent could define the Quiet Revolution, and a mere 14 percent could say why Lester Pearson had won the Nobel Peace Prize. Only 26 percent could name a war in which the United States invaded Canada (the Revolutionary War or the War of 1812), only 23 percent could identify the Loyalists, and 34 percent knew that the Acadians had been deported in the eighteenth century. The results were just as appalling on cultural questions. While 68 percent could pick Emily Carr as a Canadian artist, 30 percent thought Norman Rockwell was Canadian, as did 20 percent Allan Ginsberg, and 17 percent Tennessee Williams and Andy Warhol. Only 27 percent could identify Robert Service as Canadian, and a frightening 11 percent knew that Sir Frederick Banting had won the Nobel Prize in medicine for his discovery of insulin. And it wasn't just ancient Canadian history that drew a blank: only 16 percent could identify Marc Garneau as the first Canadian in space. Overall, Canadian youth scored just 34 percent on this test. Forty percent of those questioned, the Angus Reid Group reported, drew the proper conclusion: They did not know as much as they should.*

The results, said the Dominion Institute's director, Rudyard Griffiths, demonstrated all too clearly that Canadian youth have

9

---

* The newspapers agreed. The *Edmonton Journal* (2 July 1997) pronounced the results "a national embarrassment . . . a national disgrace . . . sheer ignorance"; the *Ottawa Citizen* (2 July 1997) editorialized that the results "inspire despair"; the *Toronto Star* (1 July 1997) found the survey's results "unthinkable"; and the *Calgary Herald* (28 June 1997) called it "frightening." Of course, it might be useful to ask how much space these and other dailies devote to covering historical and cultural matters.

a very poor knowledge of the history of the relationship between French- and English-Canadians—and much else. "The survey indicates that we have failed to impart to our youth the historical knowledge that is necessary to make informed decisions and sustain a sense of belonging."

But Canadian youth also have no Canadian reference points, few world reference points, and no basic knowledge. In his able book *In School: Our Kids, Our Teachers, Our Classrooms*, Ken Dryden noted one teacher's lament that the students in his Mississauga, Ontario, high school classroom don't know the names of provinces, capital cities, or prime ministers. They recognize Bill Clinton's name more often than Jean Chrétien's because Clinton is more likely to be mentioned on the American television shows they watch. Most young people cannot place important global historical figures such as Winston Churchill or Franklin Roosevelt; Hitler is all but unknown, Stalin and Mao Tse-tung are names they may have heard once or twice. Few are able to give the dates of the First or Second World War, or the combatants. And beyond this century, their ignorance is complete. They cannot describe, or give approximate dates for, Napoleon, the Renaissance, the Industrial Revolution, or the Norman Conquest. Nor are they any more knowledgeable about technology, literature, science, or geography.* In

10
—

---

* I acknowledge my debt here to E.D. Hirsch Jr., *Cultural Literacy* (New York 1988) which contains a sixty-page list of terms, dates, phrases, and quotations that "every American needs to know." The list is tilted heavily toward American references, but it is a good starting point for a definition of cultural literacy that adult Canadians could well read and contemplate.

effect, most students are likely to be culturally illiterate.

What is the reason for this dangerous knowledge vacuum? To Dryden, it was the fact today's students don't talk about current events around the dinner table the way his generation did. That may well be true, though it generalizes from one man's middle-class experience and neglects the explosion of media and the proliferation of computer games that absorb children today. In any case, if the dinner-table conversations have disappeared, that is all the more reason for the schools to provide the cultural/political/historical reference points that every Canadian citizen requires.

The simple truth is that Canada's public and high schools have not only stopped teaching most world history, but have also given up teaching anything we might call Canadian or national history. As a result, Canadian students rarely learn anything of their country's past or its place in world history. There is nothing by way of national standards for history, and scarcely any prospect that such standards could be agreed upon. In contrast, there have been attempts to establish such standards in the United States and in Britain, usually in response to a perceived lack of historical knowledge on the part of young people. The situation in Canadian universities is superficially better—certainly there are more Canadian historians employed and in training than at any time in our past. Still, survey courses increasingly reflect professorial interests, and those interests tend away from national and political history—the basic nuts and bolts of Canadian historical knowledge—toward such areas as gender, labour, and regional or local history.

As a result, national history has increasingly been left to journalists to write or to private foundations to promote on television or in print. Pierre Berton, Peter C. Newman, Maggie Siggins, and a few other popularizers have become the interpreters of our past for those who have the interest to read or the money to buy their books. Sometimes the journalists do this job well. Berton, for example, is probably responsible for much of the little interest there is in Canada's past. His books on the building of the Canadian Pacific Railway, Vimy, the Dionne quintuplets, and a host of other topics ranging from the Klondike to the story of Niagara Falls, are exciting tales that have consciously tried to create Canadian myths and heroes. The historical minutiae is sacrificed for the telling incident, but that is understandable, even necessary. Siggins, however, in her biography of Louis Riel, at times favoured imaginative writing over historical accuracy in her efforts to break out of the straitjacket of sober writing. Academic prose, she wrote, is "so stodgy it wilts on the page." True enough, but incorrect history is probably worse than no history at all. Popular national history in Canada, a few notable exceptions aside, is in little better shape than is academic history.

The Charles R. Bronfman Foundation has tried to improve this situation by funding *Heritage Minutes*. Beautifully produced and historically accurate, these brief television vignettes bring history to the usually vapid television viewer. By turning history into melodrama, the CRB Foundation's teleplays have unquestionably helped to popularize history with young people. The subjects covered in *Heritage Minutes* have become magnets drawing student essay writers, for example, and the series may well create a demand for a more systematic study of the past. This is all to the good, as are the historical comic books that the same foundation, in cooperation with McDonald's, is distributing widely. The first comic, on the Halifax Explosion, told Canadian children something they did not know before (though only 38 percent of them knew what the explosion was on the Dominion Institute quiz, taken after the comic was distributed).

Why have Canada's public and high schools failed to teach students about their national history? The Constitution gives control over education to the provinces, which guard their rights jealously. Quebec's quasi-federalist and separatist governments have had little interest in teaching anything but Quebec history, along with the litany of humiliations inflicted by federal governments and Anglo-Canadians that constitute the basis of Québécois grievances and nationalism. Maritime curricula, just like those in the Prairies and in British Columbia, have become ever more narrow, concentrating on the locality and the region rather than on the nation. The idea that there should be national standards in history is a political non-starter.

It is not only the Constitution that is at fault. The ministries of education in our provincial capitals and the boards of education in our cities and towns have bought holus-bolus every

13

trendy theory to emerge from faculties of education. The progressive theories of education they espouse are child-centred rather than knowledge-based. The aim is to teach problem solving and critical thinking, not content. Facts are unimportant and can always be looked up on the Internet. Those who think that content is important are slavish practitioners of old-fashioned "rote learning." The result is a generation of students who are totally ignorant of anything not beamed into their brains via TV, movies, comic books, and the Internet.

Nor is it only the young who have been robbed of their past. Very few television programs are devoted to the history of Canada—though the advent of a History Television channel may increase the quantity—and those that are produced are often biased in the extreme. Television programs on the internment of Italians suspected of Fascist sympathies or on the evacuation of Japanese Canadians from the west coast in 1942, for example, have painted brutal and bigoted wartime Canadians as the moral equivalents of those they fought in the Second World War. They were not, and only a nation robbed of its past could ever have allowed such tendentious material to air. A CBC series such as *The Valour and the Horror*, which pretended to be a dramatized documentary about Canadian participation in the Second World War, created a furore, largely because it had no context. Only federal agencies fundamentally unaware of history could have funded such programming. Worse yet, the media rallied as one to defend the writers-producers, the McKenna brothers, against the protests from veterans and parliamentarians. Freedom of speech was one of the goals these veterans had fought to preserve, and few ever expected it to be used against their courageous efforts in such a way.

The veterans, at least, knew that their history was being taken away from them. What of the millions of immigrants who have poured into, and continue to flood, Canada? Coming from Hong Kong, Somalia, Russia, Israel, Central and South America, they end up in Vancouver, Winnipeg, Toronto, and a thousand small towns. They have chosen to become Canadians. But what does Canadian society say to them? Send your children to school to learn English or French, but, have no fear, nothing about the foundations of your new country will sully their ears or minds. That Canada seems to be a nation without a past, without roots, must surprise those who listen to what their children tell them about school. They soon discover that there is little to distinguish schoolyard or teenage culture in Canada from the American culture that dominates the television screen.

And the adults? If they choose to become citizens—and many do not—they are supposed to learn the contents of a pamphlet called *A Look at Canada*, published by Citizenship and Immigration Canada in 1995. It is a thorough test, with 200 questions on history, geography, and civics. Theoretically, if applicants for citizenship study the booklet, they will know many of the essential facts about Canada.*

15

---

*A second Dominion Institute survey, released in November 1997, showed that forty-five percent of adults questioned could not meet the standard required of the citizenship test—to answer twelve of twenty questions correctly.

But the cultural challenge facing new Canadians is more seri-ous than passing a test. How do they integrate into this strange new society when the federal government, and at least one province, has its own definition of assimilation? The federal government, committed to a multiculturalism that is enshrined in the Constitution as a fundamental characteristic of the nation, promotes a very weak nationalism. Remain a Somali, a Taiwanese, a Ukrainian, or a Bolivian, the message goes, and you will be just as good a Canadian as everyone else. In effect, the message is that Canada (or English Canada, at least) has no culture. Moreover, the federal, provincial, and municipal governments will give any group money to preserve its original culture, heritage, and language. In Quebec, in sharp contrast, the provincial govern-ment controls immigration policy and follows a deliberately anti-Canadian approach as it half-heartedly tries to assimilate immigrants into francophone culture.

Ottawa's policy toward immigrants aims to encourage slow integration and to preserve the cultural mosaic in a nation that is marked by tolerance and goodwill. This approach may be well intentioned, but is it sound when no effort, other than the citi-zenship test, is made to teach newcomers that Canada is a nation with a past, with traditions, with a history? No one should be surprised, therefore, that the Croatian defence minister is a Canadian who returned "home" when the civil war erupted in Yugoslavia. No one should find it unusual that Serbian and Croatian Canadians, born in Canada, returned "home" to fight

WHAT HISTORY? WHICH HISTORY?

against the boy they went to high school with. Unthinking Canadians complacently assumed that our schools and our society had turned them all into good, bland, peace-loving Canadians. But a combination of federal multiculturalism, ignorance of an understanding of their new homeland, and the practices of progressive education had prevented them from becoming what they ought to have become: Canadians.

As a historian, I believe that an understanding of our history is important in and of itself. But history has a public purpose, too, in creating Canadians who know where they want to go in the coming years because they understand where they have been. I believe that the achievements of the past, and even the failures of years gone by, can be a source of strength to meet not only today's challenges but tomorrow's, too. If written and taught properly, history is not myth or chauvinism, just as national history is not perfervid nationalism; rather, history and nationalism are about understanding this country's past, and how the past has made our present and is shaping our future. Moreover, I believe that the past can unite us without its being censored, made inoffensive to this group or that, or whitewashed to cover up the sins of our forefathers. If our history is to achieve this great national purpose, then major changes are needed in our schools and universities.

CHAPTER 2

Teaching Ignorance: History in the Schools

"Historians," Soviet general secretary Nikita Khrushchev once said, "are dangerous people. They are capable of upsetting everything." The Russian leader understood that history matters because it is concerned with real people and with the way human lives have changed, for better or worse, over time. Small wonder it frightened Khrushchev.

The teaching of history is important because knowledge of the past is the prerequisite of political intelligence. Without history, the National Center for History in the Schools (University of California) has stated in its *National Standards for World History*, a society shares no common memory of where it has been, what its basic values are, or what past decisions have created its present circumstances. Without history, we as a nation cannot undertake any rational inquiry into the political, social, or moral issues of our society. And without historical knowledge and inquiry, we cannot achieve the informed citizenship that is essential for effective participation in the democratic process and in the fulfilment of all our democratic ideals. As the Report of Ontario's Royal Commission on Learning put it in 1995, students must have the opportunity to relate the past to the present: "Students, who will be voters, must understand . . . those links." To me, this is the key—the best of all reasons for making history a prominent part of the school curriculum.

How have Canadian schools handled this task of teaching the past to help prepare good, politically aware citizens? How have school boards and provincial governments done the job? Given the abysmal lack of basic knowledge of the Canadian past outlined in Chapter 1, the answer can only be "not very well." The general level of Canadian public debate and its contemporary focus, particularly around election times, is appalling. The untrammelled ability of premiers Jacques Parizeau and Lucien Bouchard—to cite only two politicians—to lie about recent constitutional events also suggests that few Québécois, their provincial motto *Je me souviens* notwithstanding, have any understanding of the immediate past.

The lament for the state of Canadians' knowledge of their past is not new. George Ross, the Ontario minister of education in the 1880s, wanted Canadian history to be studied and "to reach more of Canada": "As Canadians . . . we should have a Canadian history, fearless in exalting the great actions of Canada's greatest men." The histories in use across the country, he said, were "merely provincial histories, without reference to our common country."

Nothing much changed over the next seventy years, and, in 1965, A.B. Hodgetts, a history teacher at Trinity College School in Port Hope, Ontario, persuaded his board of governors to fund a National History Project. It was an assessment of Canadian civic education, a study of the impact of the schools in developing the attitudes of young Canadians toward their country. Hodgetts believed that the study of Canada should be "one of the most vital subjects taught in our schools and . . . could become a much more effective instrument . . . in the fostering of understanding among [the Canadian] people." Completed in 1968 and published under the title *What Culture? What Heritage?,* the Hodgetts study pointed to stultifying teaching methods, the boredom of students, a dearth of good published work on Canada, and a glut of textbooks that offered bland consensus versions of the Canadian past. Canadian history was widely perceived as dull, and, as a discrete subject, tended to disappear after the 1930s; after that point, high school courses became a mush of British, American, and European history.* Teachers seemed neither to know nor to care about Canadian topics, Hodgetts found, and most simply lectured from textbooks. As a result, Canadian students knew almost nothing of their own country. How then could they become good citizens?

Hodgetts's report sparked a growth in interest in Canada, something that fed on the nationalism unleashed by the centennial of

23

---

*The 1960 high school curriculum in Ontario, for example, included British history in grade 9, Canadian, U.S., and British history in grade 10, ancient and medieval history in grade 11, modern European history in grade 12, and Canadian and U.S. history in grade 13.

Confederation, Expo 67, and the emergence of Pierre Trudeau, a very different kind of Canadian leader. Soon the study of Canada was firmly ensconced in the schools and the universities. Provincial governments began to stress "Canadian studies," book publishing programs received a boost, and the Secretary of State in Ottawa offered up generous funding to supplement the money available from foundations. Everything was for the best in the best of all possible worlds. Or was it?

The boom in Canadian studies turned out to be very different from an interest in the Canadian past. Canadian studies was not a single discipline with a methodological basis; instead, it was whatever those who taught something, anything, about Canada wanted it to be—an amalgam of literature, art, current events, politics and public issues, and the environment. There was very little room here for a systematic study of the past, let alone the Canadian past. Canadian studies was seen as relevant and therefore accessible and of interest to students; Canadian history was not. Administrators, pressed by their education ministries and school boards to keep the kids interested, began to hack and slash at history courses. It was, after all, an age in which the theories of interdisciplinary education espoused in *Living and Learning*, the Ontario Hall-Dennis Report of 1968, were changing the focus of the schools to a struggle to raise the self-esteem of students. The net effect of *What Culture? What Heritage?*, a book that initially had seemed to restore a new and enlivened history to the centre of the Canadian school curriculum, instead turned out to be its death knell. In Ontario, the nation's most populous province, history became the Latin of the 1970s and 1980s: history courses as a percentage of all high school courses went from 11.4 percent in 1964 to 6.6 percent in 1981–82. Today, Ontario requires only one compulsory history course in high school, and even that (on twentieth-century Canada) is as much current events and sociology-speak as history.

The Canadian studies boom was part of a larger shift in attitudes toward learning. Developmental psychologists suggested that history was too complicated for young minds to grasp. History was so damned illogical, and it had nothing like the structure and coherence of, say, mathematics or science. At the same time, progressive educators argued that the role of schools was to foster the "development" of students, not to stuff them full of knowledge. It was all "child-centred" learning now, and testing fell into disfavour. Still others spoke about "behavioural objectives" or "accountability," and "relevance" and "self-realization" became sacred goals. In society at large (and especially after the Canadian Charter of Rights and Freedoms came into force), the emphasis shifted from community to individual rights and freedoms, and, outside Quebec, group rights began to be seen as anti-democratic. The schools reflected the shift. But almost no one called for history as a way of training the individual to be a good citizen or maintaining our heritage (except in the area of multicultural education), for fostering an understanding of where this nation and its people had been and how they had developed. To educational theorists, history was boring, irrelevant, and fit only for the slag heap, except for small nuggets that could be pulled out of the past and made useful for current concerns about racism, gender equity, and the plight of native peoples. That all this trashing of history and heritage would be destructive and divisive, rather than a uniting force, did not seem to matter.

While the new Canadian studies watered down the traditional approach to history and the progressive educators dismissed content-based learning, the provinces increasingly insisted on expanding their autonomy. Education is a provincial responsibility in Canada, and it always has been. By definition, this means there will be ten different ways of approaching the teaching of history in Canada, plus two more for the territories. Each province decides what history it will teach, when it will teach it, and what texts it will permit to be used. Obviously, the teaching of Canadian history in Quebec's French-language schools will be very different from that undertaken in Newfoundland or Saskatchewan; in fact, many provinces put their own history or that of their region first. As the federal government has no preordained role in education, it has tended not even to seek one for itself except at the university funding level and in minor ways as a facilitator. As a result, there are no measurable national standards for history (or any other subject) in Canada, no National Centre for History in the Schools, and slim prospects for the establishment of any of these things.* Nor do we have a system of advanced placement courses that let the brightest high school students do university-level work in certain subjects and get university credit for them.**

We do not even have the equivalent of the *Studienstiftung des Deutschen Volkes*, a nationwide system of income-based scholarships that go to the very best German students selected in the high schools or, for late bloomers, the universities. For four decades, the winners of this national talent search have shown up in every sector of German public life and the universities as the élite from which the nation draws its strength. Virtually every continental European nation replicates this system in one way or another. Even the United States has its National Merit Scholarships that recognize the best students in the land. It also has a National History Day competition, privately run and financed by foundations, corporations, and trade unions, that grabs the

---

* In the United States, with a similar division of powers on education, Washington's Department of Education can be more intrusive into state jurisdictions. For example, in May 1996, the department released the results of its assessment of student achievement in U.S. history. The secretary of education, bemoaning the results, called on "states and communities . . . to set challenging standards, make sure teachers are well-equipped, and then get busy with teaching and learning." The test in history was based on a framework developed by the National Assessment Governing Board, and tested 22,500 students in 1500 schools.

** The small number of students taking the International Baccalaureate program at high schools may, under certain conditions, receive university credits.

interest of American children from public and high schools each year using a designated historical topic. Our failure to create such national institutions is a major part of the Canadian problem.

As I have noted, there are substantial differences among provinces, each education ministry happily marching off in different directions to its own drummer. What this means in an increasingly mobile society is easy to imagine, with countless children repeating some content units and missing others as their parents move from Newfoundland to Alberta, or from Montreal to Vancouver.

When do the schools in the different provinces teach social studies or history and what do they require of their students?

British Columbia

K to grade 3:	within Language and Citizenship
Grades 4 to 8:	Social Studies (includes Canadian "history" content in grades 4, 5, 6, and 7)
Grades 9 to 11:	Social Studies—four credits

Alberta

Grades 1 to 9:	part of program
Grades 10 to 12:	one course each year, depending on program stream, that covers political and economic theory, ideologies, and practices

Saskatchewan

Grades 1 to 9:	part of program
Grade 10:	one course
Grade 11 or 12:	one course
Grade 12:	one course (choice of three courses in History, Native Studies, Social Studies; the third required course in grade 11 or 12 can also be in Law, Economics, or Geography)

Manitoba

Grades 1 to 8:	part of program
High school:	three-year program—two credits; four-year program—after 1998–99, two credits

Ontario

Grades 1 to 8:	part of program
Grade 7 or 8:	History and Contemporary Studies
Grade 9 or 10:	compulsory course, Contemporary Canada: Life in the Twentieth Century
OAC:	optional courses, Modern Western Civilization and/or Canada in North American Perspective

29

Quebec

Grades 1 to 8:   part of program

Grade 10:   general history

Grade 12:   History of Quebec and Canada

New Brunswick

K to grade 8:   part of program

Grades 9 to 12:   compulsory outcomes in grades 9 to 11 which can be fulfilled by Global Education, Ancient and Medieval History, and Modern History; grade 12 has optional social science courses, one of which is Canadian History

Nova Scotia

Grades 1 to 9:   included in program outcomes

Grade 9:   Maritime Studies

Grades 10 to 12:   two credits, one of which must be in Global History or Global Geography, the other from History, Geography or Economics

Prince Edward Island

Grades 1 to 9:   part of program

Grades 10 to 12:   two courses

Newfoundland

K to grade 9:   part of program

Grades 10 to 12:   two courses from each of the following areas: Canadian Studies, World Studies, and Economic Education*

Buried somewhere in that list is whatever Canadian children learn about their own country. In Ontario, for example, the ministry's twelve Aims of History and Contemporary Studies say little about learning and much about unabashed social engineering. The first aim is that students should "develop confidence in themselves and in their ability to deal with problems in academic and everyday life and to make sound personal, educational, and career choices." This is the first goal of the teaching of history? Never fear: the ninth aim of the twelve listed is to "acquire knowledge of historical and contemporary societies in the form of facts, concepts, and generalizations."

What does the curriculum amount to? In four provinces, one Canadian history course (sometimes only one term long) is required to graduate from high school. Two provinces require two such history courses. Four—Alberta, Saskatchewan, Nova Scotia, and Newfoundland—require no Canadian history at all. In other words, where history of any kind is compulsory, it will probably, but not necessarily, be Canadian history. Even where a course

31

---

* Based on data gathered by the Curriculum, Learning, and Teaching Branch of the Ontario Ministry of Education and up to date as of October 1996. Virtually all provinces have their curricula under review.

purports to teach about the Canadian past, it will almost certainly be larded with current events, civics, and pop sociology. No one should be surprised that Canadian students know so little about their past, or that their parents, most of whom went to school after the 1960s' revolution in education sacrificed content for the sake of the "whole child," are so poorly informed about their country.

Worse yet, some provinces are watering down the requirements still further. In Manitoba, three social studies credits were required until recently in the four-year high school program; the Progressive Conservative government of Gary Filmon has announced plans to reduce the number to two credits. Canadian history, which had been included in the required courses, was removed, a change that provoked a testy debate in the legislature in 1995 between the education minister, Linda McIntosh, and the New Democratic Party's critic, Jean Friesen, a professional historian. McIntosh countered that Friesen was incorrect in claiming that history was being downgraded. Yes, it was true that only language arts and mathematics were to be compulsory in grade 12, but history would "receive renewed emphasis in the first ten years of schooling." "We are moving," McIntosh continued, "to a model where content that was taught in 12 years will now be taught in 10 and that [sic] the increased emphasis on Canadian history and social studies will take place earlier, in more detail." Whether students aged seven to fourteen can grasp important historical concepts, whether twelve years of content squashed into ten will be sufficient to instil a basic understanding of the nation's past, did not seem to trouble the minister, though it certainly troubled Jean Friesen—as it does me. The Dominion Institute's 1997 survey of historical knowledge showed Manitoban youth ranking sixth in the nation, nothing to brag about; the new policies will certainly lower even this dismal success rate. Still, it is unfair to pick on Ms. McIntosh and her government; they are typical of all ministers and all governments in Canada, whether they be Liberal, Progressive Conservative, Parti Québécois, or NDP.

The reason is clear. It is not really the ministers who make policy but the bureaucrats. The professional educators who dominate the education ministries in the provinces remain fixated on the theory of progressive education, on remedying societal ills such as sexism and racism, and on making students feel good about themselves. Whatever the criticism of those who believe otherwise, content remains second to process—a distant second. Because it is, by definition, full of content, history is no priority, especially when it is compared with trendier subjects. As an editorial in the *Ottawa Citizen* put it, "generic 'serious issues' courses permit the displacement of Vimy Ridge by Brazilian rain-forest logging, Sir Wilfrid Laurier by Third World child labor."

In Quebec, the same child-centred ideology prevails, but additional ideological aims are also being pressed by the Parti Québécois government. What is most striking to anyone reading Quebec curricular materials is the overt stress on Quebec.

33

The compulsory grade 12 course on the history of Quebec and Canada is, at least, honest enough in its title to indicate where the emphasis is to be placed; the general objectives are clearly drafted to meet "the needs of students in the present context of Quebec society," to ensure that they all understand the (inevitable?) evolution of Quebec society. To judge by the curricular materials, Canadian history is merely the alien backdrop against which events in francophone Quebec occur. Scarcely any attempt is made to compare life, issues, and events in Quebec with those elsewhere in Canada. If it happened in Quebec, in other words, it's important; if it didn't, it's not—unless *les maudits Anglais* humiliated *les pauvres Québécois* yet again.

Moreover, Canada is almost always presented as a single unit, an English-speaking entity perpetually united in word, thought, and deed. After 1939, Canada all but disappears from the course of study, which focuses on events within the province. The Dominion Institute's survey found that Quebec students had the lowest score in answering questions about Canadian history, but on Quebec questions or questions of special interest to French-English relations they did relatively well. What was not broken out in the poll were results in Quebec by language. Columnist William Johnson has said that English-language students fail the grade 12 history course in larger numbers than do francophones, something he attributes to a curriculum with the "systemic view of our common history

34

implied by so many of the questions." Originally prepared in French and translated, the questions in 1997 talked of "the economic and social liberation of French Canadians" and noted that Anglo-Quebeckers were imperialist "business people or employers" who opposed any recognition of the French language. The examination also stated as fact that "the federal government patriated the Constitution without Quebec's consent"—a loose interpretation, to say the least. Perhaps the reason English-speaking students fail in such large numbers has more to do with the biases of the questions and the difficulty teachers have in spouting the authorized version of the past. And if francophones do well, it might be because their teachers, whose unions are heavy separatist supporters, preach the party line that Quebec has a collective history and forms a nation. The point, as the Dominion Institute survey shows, is that Quebec's policy of stressing its own history has worked, and that Quebec City's education bureaucrats have shrewdly positioned the sole compulsory Quebec and Canada history course in grade 12, aiming it at students who are likely to be eligible voters within a year.

Quebec's recommended and approved textbooks provide the underpinnings for the compulsory history course. A paper by the Université de Montréal's Monique Nemni, presented at the 1996 Learned Societies meeting, focused on the high school history texts. To cite one example:

35

I find the absence of crucial words [in a section on the October Crisis of 1970 from the most widely used text] extremely interesting. Nowhere do we read that the FLQ is a group of terrorists that used bombs that killed innocent people, that [kidnapped British trade commissioner James] Cross and [Quebec Labour minister Pierre] Laporte were hostages. Laporte is not assassinated, he is simply found dead (Did he get a heart attack?). There is no blackmail, no turmoil in Montreal. The population is not scared. Nobody is found guilty, although the members of the FLQ are imprisoned and exiled. Which members of the FLQ were imprisoned or exiled? All of them, even the ones that did not take part in the abduction and assassination?

Nemni concludes that "nationalism in Quebec is not propagated in a haphazard way by individual teachers. It starts at the Ministry level, and it permeates the textbooks." Such manipulation has been so whether the Liberals or the Parti Québécois formed the government.

On the other hand, Québécois students are every bit as present-minded as students in Toronto or Calgary. They are hardly stuffed with history, any more than are students elsewhere in the country. How much propaganda permeates a youthful mind more interested in Celine Dion than in Dollard des

Ormeaux or the patriation of the Constitution? There is, moreover, a healthy debate in the province about the way history is taught. A working group recommended to the Ministry of Education that history be a compulsory subject in all grades; the Estates-General on Education that reported in 1996 did not go so far, but it did want more stress on history; and in June 1997 the minister of education agreed to increase the history requirement. All this attention suggests that historians in Quebec feel the same despair as do their colleagues in Canada, though they have had more success than their peers elsewhere. Most of the shouting, however, is directed at the pedagogical methods employed, not the content—although the 1996 report *Se souvenir et devenir* did call for special efforts at acculturating immigrants, both children and adults. There might be something there worth emulating in the rest of Canada.

The Quebec curriculum highlights the different ways that Canadian history is taught in the various regions. In Quebec, the Conquest of 1759 is featured; in the West, it is touched on only lightly. The same is true for the Quiet Revolution. Yet Québécois learn little about western developments, including settlement, the rise of protest parties, and western alienation. The teaching of Canadian history in the schools, like Canada itself, is regionalized, fragmented along geographical lines. The idea that Canada is bigger than the provinces, that national issues and national projects have mattered, is scarcely mentioned. National history, the national context, is provided only incidentally. Quebec, in other words, is little different from British Columbia or Nova Scotia, except in the political aims that inspire its teaching.

In addition to the provincial spin that is put on the study of our past, other factors affect classroom learning. In virtually every city in the country, there are large numbers of recent immigrant children who speak little or no English and whose parents are not citizens. Some come from nations with similar cultures that value education, but many don't. Some of these children, their minds and emotions back in their homelands at least for the first few years, have not the slightest interest or background in Canadian history, and teachers must scramble to find ways to make the material being taught meaningful. Not surprisingly, the teacher must devote attention to English comprehension and to reading and writing skills, as well as to help students adapt to North American life with all its shocks and temptations. As one public school teacher told me, "The reality of the classrooms and schools is that many children . . . could not handle the teaching of history, as they struggle even to master Dr. Seuss books." The struggle that teachers in the big cities face, trying to meet the ministry's and the school boards' demands while teaching children from a hundred different nations, deserves our sympathy and support.

Of course, it's not only the recent arrivals who can neither read nor write. Given declining literacy in general, and despite the most recent United Nations' data that suggest that 99 percent of Canadians are literate, functional literacy is declining dramatically. Canadian-born students are all too often non-readers whose idea of education is watching television or surfing the Internet, and who seem incapable of absorbing information that is not presented in two-minute chunks with explosive graphics and volume. The result, despite the best efforts of many dedicated teachers, is a broad-brush treatment of the past that can do nothing more than teach a few skills (note taking, writing a paragraph) and a smattering of content.

The texts used in courses today, while varying widely in quality, are in general surprisingly good. Some are pitched at English as a second language students and have a simplified language base and lighter content. Others use straightforward language and present history in some depth—though J.B. Cruxton and W.D. Wilson's *Spotlight Canada,* a popular text in high school Canadian history courses, was noticeably glitzed up in appearance but watered down in language and detail between its first and third editions. No textbook writer has ever been penalized in sales for underestimating student abilities, as the most popular readers in many classrooms demonstrate. The *Canadiana Scrapbook Series,* to cite but one example, is a set of pamphlets whose title precisely describes their format. In less than fifty pages, students get newspaper clippings, photographs of leaders and ordinary people, posters, tables, and primary documents, all presented attractively in a way that should hold their interest. But no textual material is included in the scrapbooks to put it all in context. In effect, what these books do is replicate a TV program in print: they present brief bursts of information in a slam-bang fashion. All that's missing is sound effects—and undoubtedly the CD-ROMs are already in production to provide the explosive bursts of noise to grab the students' attention. Still, the scrapbooks are better than no information at all.

The texts must also pander to provincial guidelines, and it is not only Quebec that is guilty in this respect. The role of women, for example, is a popular subject with ministries of education and school boards across the country, and rightly so. It should not be surprising, therefore, that Allan Hux and Fred Jarman's *Canada: A Growing Concern* devotes much more space to women's role in the First World War than to that of farmers, workers, and even the federal government. Still, all women are treated as a single group—rural, urban, middle class or working class, French or English speaking, or immigrant in origin—generic Canadian women of the 1914–18 variety.

Similarly, in J.B. Cruxton and R.J. Walker's *Community Canada*, a full-length textbook designed for grade 7 and 8 history classes to cover pre-Confederation Canada, there are more than a hundred pages on "Native Communities." The authors' attempt not only to treat each of the major native peoples one after another, but to carry the story to the present.* The result is a simplistic treatment of prejudice and a disregard for chronology,

40

---

* As this example suggests, the history of Canada's Aboriginal peoples is covered at some length in the schools in every province. So it should be, though we might benefit from fewer latherings of guilt on the events of the past.

the basic tool of historical study. Much better in this regard is *Canada Revisited: A Social and Political History of Canada to 1911* by Penney Clark and Roberta McKay.

In the social studies classes in the lower grades of the public schools, few textbooks are used; instead picture books (along with videos and teachers' guides) carry the load. While there are many good picture books on narrow social history topics such as regionalism, women's issues, multiculturalism, and native history, there is very little that presents political history in its broadest sense. The few books that are available, one teacher lamented, are "usually so dated and visually boring that teachers wouldn't dare attempt to use them in the classroom." Perhaps there is scope here for a publisher to seize the opportunity.

But should we blame the textbook writers? The teachers who prepare the texts (and few university professors today write for the public school or high school market) are trying to meet the requirements that are laid down by the provincial ministries. Only in this way can they get on the list of acceptable books that may be used for instruction. In each province, committees of bureaucrats ruthlessly vet the manuscripts of texts, demanding politically correct language, insisting on adding this and delet- ing that, and, overall, producing the blandest of mush. It is not the textbook writers who should be blamed for whatever flaws are found in their books but the officials in the education ministries, and the ministers and premiers who direct them. I might also add that the voters who elected the politicians who have done such damage to our schools and to a generation of students are entitled to their full measure of blame.

What can be done in the face of the provincial know-nothings? I believe that what is needed is a major effort to establish national standards for history in our schools. To say this is far easier than to accomplish it, given the constitutional control of education vested in the provinces. Even so, every opinion survey, every study over the last twenty years, has demonstrated that Canadians want to know more about their history and heritage and are very uneasy about the ways in which the schools are teaching these subjects. There is an opportunity here, if Ottawa has the courage to grab it.

In the United States in the early 1990s, there was a significant attempt to establish national history standards for teaching United States and world history to meet the same appalling gaps in knowledge among American students that trouble me among Canadian youth. Developed at the National Center for History in the Schools, the U.S. standards provoked a storm of controversy because, critics said, they were politically correct, replete with divisive multiculturalism, and obsessed with issues (racism, McCarthyism, the mistreatment of Aboriginal peoples) that some on the left or the right always saw as anti-American. The standards were stalled, perhaps never to come forward again. The key points, however, are that history was considered important enough to be argued about; that leading scholars, commentators, and congressional representatives joined the debate; and that the way the American past was taught was recognized as critical to national development.

How different it is in Canada! There has never been an attempt to establish national standards here and, should there be, there would probably be just as little agreement as in the United States. Canadians appear to have concluded that history is unimportant at best or divisive at worst; in either case, it is not something worth fighting about or worth teaching. Yet, Canada can never be a strong nation (or even two nations) if it does not teach its past to its people. The country needs a nationally based history curriculum with its content defined for each grade, and with publishers given specific targets for their texts to meet. To protect teachers' autonomy, the teaching strategies and methods of assessment must be left to the classroom practitioners.

How might national standards for Canadian history be developed? First, they should aim to give students two things: historical understanding (or content) that can define what students know about the history of their country and the world—understanding sufficient to provide the historical perspectives required to analyse contemporary issues; and the skills necessary to evaluate evidence, develop comparative and causal analyses, and construct historical arguments on which informed decisions about contemporary life might be based.

Second, criteria must be developed to guide the specific content standards, and should include some or all of the following:

- Standards should be intellectually rigorous and aim to promote questioning, not passive absorption of facts.

43

- Standards must be founded on chronology, the only organizing method that fosters the appreciation of pattern and causality.
- Standards must stress techniques of reading, understanding, and researching the past.
- Standards should strike a balance between broader themes and the study of specific events, ideas, movements, and people.
- Standards for Canadian history should reflect both the country's diversity *and* its commonalities.
- Standards for Canadian history should contribute to citizenship education through the development of understanding about our common civic identity and shared values, and through the analysis of major policy issues.
- Standards for Canadian history must address the historical roots of our democracy, the continuing development of Canada's ideals and institutions, and the struggle to narrow the gap between ideals and practices.
- Standards for Canadian history must reflect the global context in which Canada developed.
- Standards for Canadian history must include national history, as well as regional and local history, and such areas of culture as religion, science and technology, politics and government, social history, literature, and the arts.

44

To suggest the detailed content of Canadian history standards would be outside the scope of this book, except to say that the focus should be on the ordinary people *and* the leaders, on the failures *and* the successes of our governments and people. Given the current focus of the research, writing, and teaching of Canadian history in the universities and schools on the flaws in Canadian society, this suggestion is more radical than is at first apparent. But the criteria above, loosely derived from the standards proposed for the United States, suggest some clear directions.

The teaching of history must be intellectually rigorous, something that it currently is not. Intellectual rigour has come to be seen as élitist in our public schools, and efforts to press children to work hard, to struggle to master complex materials, are frowned on as favouring the most intelligent and fostering unhealthy competition among students. If we fail to educate the brightest of our students well, if the rich opt out of the public school system and pay the high costs involved in sending their children to private schools with supposedly higher academic standards, then we truly will have an élitist system—and a dangerous one. To stultify learning in the public school system out of a misplaced fear of élitism is a route to national suicide, and not only in the teaching of history.

History must also teach the ways to assess evidence. Students must learn how to interpret documentation, understand narrative, evaluate conflicting perspectives, and do research. Those techniques have relevance in every other aspect of education and life. But skills, however important they be, are not and cannot be made a substitute for content. There are some who argue that it

45

scarcely matters what history is taught, so long as the right methods are learned. David Pratt told the Canadian Historical Association in 1983 that in the elementary schools, "what is of main importance in history is the skills of handling evidence . . . The names, dates, places and events are pegs on which to hang arguments and concepts concerning human ideas and motivation, conflict and synergy, justice and freedom." If there were still five compulsory history courses in the high schools, one might reasonably make this argument, but at a time when most students are exposed to only one or even a half course in Canadian history, such methodological nonsense stressing process above content is simply destructive. Teach the method, by all means, but we must teach content as well. Increasingly, our public and high schools have failed to do so.

Content is not mere facts, drummed into tender little minds under the relentless pounding of rote learning. Content—even the date of the Quebec Act, Confederation, or the Battle of Vimy Ridge, or the name of the first prime minister—is cultural capital, a basic requirement of life that every Canadian needs to comprehend the daily newspaper, to watch the TV news or a documentary, or to argue about politics and cast a reasonably informed vote. In an increasingly complex and immediate world, cultural capital must also include some knowledge of Europe, Africa, and Asia, too. Without some factual basis, some understanding of why Afghanis, Bosnians, or Congolese act as they do, Canadians will never make sense of what is happening around them. A knowledge of fact and an understanding of trends form the critical elements of our society's public discourse, and if Canadians do not have cultural capital in common, the fragmentation of our society is inevitable.

The teaching of this content must be based on chronology, the basic tool of history. By putting events in order, we can begin to comprehend why, if *this* event happened in 1789 or 1914, *that* result followed in 1793 or 1919. Too much teaching in schools today takes a module of history and puts it before students to be digested, without much awareness of how it fits within a larger context. Just like Brad, to whom I referred in the preface, students can move from an examination of gender inequity in the seventeenth century to a consideration of racism in the mid-twentieth century. Such an approach can never make clear how and why events occurred, or provide a sense of the forces that directed and affected those who lived and struggled in a past era.

Nor can Canadian students begin to understand how their country developed if its history is isolated from general world history. In Ontario, grade 9 history used to be devoted to British history, a subject put in place because of imperial and pro-British nostalgia, but also and more significantly because Canada's institutions in large part sprang from British models. Over the years, educators began to argue that in a multicultural Canada, teaching British history to all students favoured one ethnic group over the others. This was foolish reasoning that ignored the historical roots of the Canadian nation, but it prevailed, with the result that British history disappeared, and students no longer understand where our parliamentary system came from and how we have changed the Westminster model—to cite a single example.

Ideally, Canadian students would all begin historical study with the history of the ancient world and follow events chronologically through to the present. They would learn how Canada grew and changed within a global context, understanding the forces that shaped the settlement of the new world, the conquest of the Aboriginal peoples, and the subsequent creation of new societies. They would understand why Canada was involved in the European wars from the sixteenth century through to the Second World War. They would know how Canada's relations with the United States developed in a world of changing superpowers, and they might even learn why this nation today plays such a large role in United Nations' peacekeeping. Above all, they would learn history systematically, rather than in a vague, unstructured exercise. For all its undoubted flaws, the 1960 Ontario history curriculum—and those in British Columbia, Manitoba, Nova Scotia, and every other province—went much further toward achieving these goals than anything currently offered anywhere in Canada.

I recognize that such a sensible approach (even though it is followed as a matter of course in good British public schools, but not any longer in U.K. state schools) is unlikely ever to return to Canada's educational systems. The best we can hope is that Canadian history will be taught in detail, in a chronological fashion, with continuous, clear reference to the international context in which events here occurred. Ideally, it should be taught compulsorily in the higher grades and not, as is usually the case, to eleven to fourteen year olds who are too young to grasp the real issues. The young should get history as story; the older students should begin to analyse what happened and why. Without such aims, our history becomes all but meaningless.

An effort to secure national standards is worth the effort. It might not succeed but, as in the United States, the discussion, the arguments, and the contradictory interpretations of the past that would be sure to emerge will help make Canadians understand who they are and why their past matters.

There are some small signs that history is beginning to make some impact on the public consciousness. In Ontario, the Progressive Conservative government appears determined to press ahead with a major school curricular reform. Measurable standards, system-wide testing, a return to streaming students, and more compulsory courses appear to be the aim, and the minister until October 1997, John Snobelen, even mentioned in his speeches the need to teach Canadian history. Unfortunately, these changes are being proposed after a major series of school board restructurings, downsizings, and teacher strikes that have left the province reeling. In the circumstances, whether Snobelen's successor can move the bureaucrats, whether he can carry the teachers (and even more important, the teachers' unions) with him is unclear. Current indications are that curriculum review will produce more of the same at both the primary and the secondary levels, the review committees having a marked bias against history as a distinct subject.

The one certainty is that parents, alarmed by how little their children know, will support any measures that promise to improve the quality and content of education. If Ontario can reverse the precipitous decline of its public school system, if it can bring its students up to the stellar level achieved by Alberta's schools in the Third International Mathematics and Science Study (in which Ontario students were last among the five provinces participating) and the Dominion Institute's historical knowledge survey,* then the rest of the country may be encouraged to follow. History, and especially Canadian history, must be part of the core curriculum in every province.

---

* Although Alberta's history scores were nothing to cheer too loudly about, the province's youth scored 40 points out of 100 in the Dominion Institute's survey, a modest few points ahead of the 34 points that was the depressing average mark for the 1104 young men and women who took the test. Forty percent of those questioned said they didn't know as much as they should, and perhaps this realization is the beginning of self-awareness.

CHAPTER 3

Professing Trivia: The Academic Historians

If provincial education departments, school boards, and history teachers have let their students and their country down, so too have universities and their professors of history. Party politics and the theories of progressive educators may have determined that schools should teach children to achieve self-respect rather than to learn anything, but in university history departments the situation is just as bleak.

Universities are curious creatures. They are almost wholly funded by the provincial governments and student tuition fees, but their paymasters have little control over what they do or how they do it. The administrations preach their autonomy and independence from the paymaster, and sometimes they even exercise it. Faculty members, unionized or not, jealously protect their right to determine the courses they teach as well as the content. In the name of "academic freedom," they study whatever they choose without fear of losing their jobs.

An ideal situation for professors: they teach the subjects they like and say what they will, arguing always that this or that body of knowledge is essential for their students to master. In truth, professors are the merest of mere mortals, and their decisions on courses and course content are reached through small-group politics and individual whim, much like other decisions that shape our lives. History departments usually have a chair who administers and presides; in days past, the chair was the true head of the department and could direct, but this is no longer the case. The assembled faculty will decide on broad areas to be covered in the curriculum, work out what is necessary for an ordinary degree and an honours BA, and lay down the standards for graduate degrees, all subject to the overriding policies of the university.

Specialization is a critical element of university education in an era that frowns on generalists. Most universities determine the number of courses or credits that a student must have for a BA in history, but few universities go further. The history department will say, for example, that the student should take— whatever the specialty—at least one course in methodology, one course in ancient or medieval history, and one course outside the history of North America. There will be four, six, or eight history courses, depending on the institution, but almost no college will mandate that a student must study Canadian history to graduate. That would be viewed by all faculty members, especially those teaching non-Canadian subjects, as interference of the most crass kind—and besides, the students had Canadian

54

history in public and high school, didn't they? As we have seen, they probably did not, but compulsory courses, and especially required Canadian courses, are almost never ordained. Students can graduate from a Canadian university with an honours degree in history, an MA, and a PhD, without ever coming into contact with the history of their own nation.

If the student decides it is important to know the history of the society in which he or she lives, there will usually be a vast array of courses and approaches from which to choose. Even the meanest institution feels obliged to cover the basic chronology of Canadian history; even the weakest offers lecture courses with tutorials and seminars for more specialized work. But who and what determines the courses that will be offered and their content?

The details of curriculum planning are determined in meetings of the specialists. The European historians, the Americanists, and the medievalists will all decide what courses will be taught, what they will contain, and who will teach them. The Canadian specialists do this, too. In most Canadian university history departments, there are more Canadian specialists than anything else, as there should be. Most departments will have pre- and post-Confederation teachers, some will have experts on Aboriginal history, and all will have professors who teach social history, a broad area that encompasses gender studies, labour history, urban history, economic history, demographics, ethnic and immigration history, as well as local or regional history, and the history of medicine or business. There will also probably be an expert or two in political or constitutional history.

A generation ago, the Canadianists in virtually every department would have been very differently organized. Most would have been the political and constitutional specialists, and most would have focused their research and teaching on national politics. There were biographers and experts on elections or chronological periods, and specialists on Sir John A. Macdonald or the Laurier period. A few worked intensively on Canadian-American political, diplomatic, and economic relations, or on the Canadian government in the Second World War. There were almost no professors teaching women's history or native history, few working on the regions or the provinces, and only the beginnings of specialization in other genres. Canadian history, professionally speaking, was a backwater. As more students went overseas or to the United States to do graduate work, however, they came home with new interests and new approaches. They wanted to write about ordinary people, not the leaders, the boring old white males who dominated the traditional history. "What about the workers?" they asked, and labour history sprang up, dedicated to the writing of history that did not present the story from the viewpoint of the capitalist exploiters. "What about the women?", and women's history developed. What about the cities and towns, the Maritimes and the West, the immigrants and the sojourners, the gays and the lesbians, the businesses and the fluctuations in the business cycle? Could the quantitative techniques used in the "hard" social sciences also be applied to the study of the past? Under the impact of the new, the dominance of political and constitutional history shattered, never to be restored. There can be no doubt whatsoever that these developments were long overdue.

The best example of the "new" Canadian history can be found in the introduction to the first edition of *History of the Canadian Peoples*, a popular two-volume university text whose second volume was written by Margaret Conrad and Alvin Finkel, with assistance from Veronica Strong-Boag. It is self-consciously a history of the Canadian peoples—note the politically correct use of the plural—that is deliberately intended to be about the common folk, not the kings, prime ministers, and élites. As its preface proudly states, it is a history written to counter that produced in the past by "a small élite of educated white men to be read by others like themselves." It is not a history of war and political developments "in which they and their peers participated," nor is it a history written "from the point of view of the people who dominated such events." Moreover, it is not a history written from a central Canadian perspective. Instead, this is history from the points of view of women, the working class, minorities, and regions. This is history as "an arena in which classes, ethnic groups, and individual men and women struggled to control the values that shaped their collective lives." The new history uses the new methodologies imported from geography, demography, economics, political science, sociology, anthropology, archaeology, and psychology, as well as the theoretical perspectives of Marxism, feminism, and postmodernism to produce what is claimed to be a more comprehensive portrait of Canadian society.

But like all innovations, there can be too much of a good thing. Not surprisingly, the practitioners of the new approaches, as the introduction to *History of the Canadian Peoples* suggests, quickly developed a scorn for the old ways and their middle-class practitioners, and they fought for control in their departments and their professional associations. They achieved it.*

The old was swept away almost completely. The new historians effectively and efficiently took over Canadian history, setting up new journals or assuming control of the old. They ascended to the presidencies of the scholarly associations and set up specialized associations of their own, driving out all those who did not follow the mandated approach. They rewarded themselves with the prizes and fellowships that were under the control of historians—though they did less well with awards that were controlled by more broadly based organizations. They

*Canada was not unique in this historical trend. In the United States in the 1960s, 1970s, and 1980s, many historians practised a "blame the U.S. for everything" school of historical diplomatic analysis that dovetailed perfectly with a broader attack on the worth and values of Western civilization. The status quo was denounced and blame was allocated, but nothing was offered in its place, except perhaps a warmed-over Marxism that had little or no support anywhere, and certainly none outside the universities.

took over the hiring processes in their departments, thus guaranteeing that they could replicate themselves at will, and they trained graduate students to do the kind of work they preached and practised. They freely denounced the political historians as second rate, teaching unimportant subjects and publishing shoddy work.

As the old white males rallied themselves and fought back, the resulting war produced heavy casualties, much bloodshed, and vast expenditures of time and effort. The political historians believed that narrative was important, that chronology mattered, and that the study of the past could not neglect the personalities of the leaders and the nations they led. The social historians had no interest in the history of the "élites" and almost none in political history, except to denounce the repressiveness of Canadian governments and business. It was far more important to study how the workers resisted industrialization, the Marxist historians claimed; to investigate how birth control was practised before the Pill, feminist historians maintained; or to document gay men's experiences in Toronto's bath houses, than to study the boring lives of prime ministers, the efforts of the Canadian Corps in the Great War, or the Quiet Revolution in Quebec. Blame had to be allocated. Canada was guilty of genocide against the Indians, the bombing of Germany, the ecological rape of the landscape, and so on. Their aim was to use history, or their version of it, to cure white males of their sense of superiority. As French intellectual Alain Finkielkraut put it, "to give other people back their pride[:] Bring down the offenders, raise up the offended."*

The struggle for the past first began in Canada in labour history. The field was small and, until about 1970, it was usually studied in a narrow focus. What was the Winnipeg General Strike about? What kinds of trade unions organized and why did they succeed or fail? But such issues were unimportant to the new breed of labour historians who burst upon the field. They had new questions. What were the workers thinking in 1919 as they rose as one against their oppressors? What was the value of the general strike as a weapon? These differences in approach may sound trivial, but the battle between the Marxists and the non-Marxists, the new and the old labour historians, was vicious. There was only one way to study and teach the history of labour, and any form of attack against the old and traditional historians was justified. If research grant applications were sent for appraisal to the "wrong" individual, they were assessed negatively, with sweeping critiques of methodology. Book reviews verged on the personal, and simple survey articles on the state of

* Increasingly, social historians have no interest in what H.V. Nelles coldly called "the nation as a unit of analysis in social history." At York University, he noted correctly, "for a decade or more, graduate students have been taught 'Western Social History'" covering all of the Western world ("American Exceptionalism: A Double-Edged Sword," *American Historical Review* 102 (June 1997): 754n). In other words, social history is social history, and Canadian variants have no special importance or claim to be taught.

the field became great battlegrounds for the destruction of the enemy. A graduate student, unlucky enough to be on the "wrong" side, could expect a rough ride in examinations.

Both sides fought with vigour, but no one can compete with Marxists in vituperation. The old-style institutional labour historians were either driven out or left the field to seek new areas to work in. The Marxists had complete control of the labour history field, including the journals and the students, and they maintain it still, notwithstanding the discrediting of Marxism everywhere in the world. The universities, sheltered from the real world, continue to protect their Marxists.

Women's historians followed suit and launched their struggle to ensure that the history of woman received its proper place. And so it should. For years, women were ignored not only in the writing of Canadian history but in the teaching, too. But the effort to rectify a wrong, as always, went too far. As Roger Hall put it delicately in the *Globe and Mail,* the heart of the change effected by women's history "has been to redirect the focus of the study of human experience away from political-economic roots toward social and cultural ones." Indeed, the political-economic roots scarcely matter any longer to entire schools of Canadian historians.

At the same time, women historians pored through textbooks to determine sex equity content. One 1987 study reported on the results: "Researchers read each of [66] books from cover to cover, noting, by page, references to women and/or girls and to 'women's issues' such as the fight for suffrage, child and infant mortality or prohibition . . . passing references . . . were also noted by page. We then calculated the extent of sex equitable content using each reference, even those of a single word." None of the surveyed books met the requirements of the sex equity policy of the Ontario Ministry of Education, and the researchers concluded that women had been marginalized by historians. Other provinces conducted similar surveys that produced equivalent results. No one seemed to care that most of Canada's history had been made by men, however unfair that might have been, and that any overt attempt to write more women into history might distort the past.

The same story with minor or major variations occurred in other fields of Canadian history, as ethnic historians, regional historians, and others counted up references and paraded their indignation. So sharp was the sense of hurt, the determination to battle against the received version of the past, that today's sensible graduate students, desperately seeking teaching posts after they get their doctorates, worry whether to choose sides in the struggles in Canadian history or to stand aloof. Most of them appear to agree, whatever their personal decision, that fighting within and between specialties does no one any good. The all-or-nothing mindset of their compartmentalized professors horrifies and frightens them. Isn't the university a community of scholars? they ask. Shouldn't survey courses, at least, try to weave all the new perspectives, including those in political history, into a seamless web that teaches first-year students about *all* of Canadian history? Put in the women, the immigrants, and the workers, by all means, but why throw out the politicians, businessmen, and soldiers?

It is stunning to see the scorn in which the "old" national history is held by the practitioners of the "new." An average Canadian might think that Canada's relationship with the United States is historically important. Or Canada's foreign policy toward Britain, France, and China, to name only three nations with which we have traded in the past. Or the development of Canada's public service, the Canadian Forces, and major public policies. Or the lives and administrations of prime ministers and premiers. But such subjects are ignored by the new historians. Not only are they old hat, but they pale beside the need to understand questions of labour militancy, gender, and the lives of obscure social reformers. It is somehow considered improper to study a white male prime minister, but the first Jewish dentist in Nova Scotia or an unknown female doctor in northern Alberta is worth a book. Why Canadian history should not include both the great men and the workers and women does not seem to occur to the defenders of the new history, who have revealed themselves to be far more hidebound and rigid than those they denounce. Such disputes are like theological discussions of the number of angels who can dance on the head of a pin, except that these debates are important, for they determine how Canadians understand their past. As the *Globe and*

Mail's Jeffrey Simpson said: "History departments now largely teach particularistic histories of people defined by region, locality, gender or ethnicity. Political history is considered passé in many quarters, as is history on the grand scale. Micro-history has taken over, galvanizing some, boring most."

These debates inevitably have their effect on PhD students as they watch their professors wage their battles and commit their little murders. When the Canadian specialists, secure in their narrow compartments, meet in their departmental planning sessions, it is the new that dominates. The social historians fight fiercely to have more labour history than women's history taught. Only if the few surviving political historians raise their heads to plead for more do the social historians unite to swat them down.

Increasingly the old subject areas will be taught less and less, or even not at all. At St. John's Memorial University in 1994–95, the calendar listed twenty-one Canadian courses, of which six were social history, two were labour, six were regional, three were native, one was ethnic/immigration, four were economic, and none was political. In the graduate history program of the University of Ottawa in 1994–95, twenty-seven courses were offered, including one on labour, five on social history, eight on regional history, and only two on political history. The University of Toronto offered its undergraduates twenty-seven courses on Canadian history, including five on social history, two on immigration, one each on native, women's, urban, economic, and labour, three on regional, and two on political history (these last in the International Relations program). Only in western Canada did political history courses remain in substantial numbers in university calendars. The University of Calgary offered eight political history courses out of thirty; the University of Alberta, fourteen out of thirty-eight; the University of Saskatchewan, ten out of seventeen; and the University of British Columbia, eight out of sixteen.* What is clear, whatever the number of political history courses, is that national history—the history of Canada as a nation and a collectivity—is taught scarcely at all except in broad survey courses usually pitched at first- and second-year students. In the Maritimes and Quebec, especially, the history of the region prevails. Even where the calendars list Post-Confederation History as a survey course, often the content will omit all but the most cursory account of national events. There are professors who brag that the names of Sir Wilfrid Laurier or Mackenzie King are never uttered in their survey courses, so fixed are they on the history of Franco-Ontarians, the history of contraceptive use and abortion, or the social history they espouse.

The result is that university graduates, like those who enter the labour force directly from high school, emerge into the marketplace culturally illiterate, ignorant of the basic details

---

*It is important to note that many courses straddle several fences simultaneously (and are counted in each) and that course descriptions in university calendars are notoriously unrevealing and unreliable. The figures above, with the best will in the world, can only be estimates.

about their nation and their society that every thinking citizen requires. Yes, they may have historiographical skills that render them every bit as well trained as German, American, or French graduates; but unlike almost all those nations' graduates, the Canadians know little about their own country's history.

Happily, there are signs that many students are not pleased with this approach. The elective social history courses are usually seminars with small numbers. Courses in political history, military history, or foreign policy, where they are still taught, are often very large and extraordinarily popular. Military history courses at the University of New Brunswick, Wilfrid Laurier University, the University of Western Ontario, and the University of Calgary are pacesetters in their departments, with waiting lists for entry to some classes. The students are voting with their feet, and they seem interested in learning who John A. Macdonald was and why he drank, what Canada's involvement was in the world wars and how conscription drove French and English Canadians apart, and what role Mike Pearson played in the Suez Crisis of 1956.

Why does it matter if university students can shun their nation's history? Many of the history teachers in the primary and secondary schools and in the universities are drawn from these graduates. They teach what they know, and, in too many cases, they know nothing at all about the national history of Canada. Obviously, social history is a critical part of that history and it must be taught, but so too is national and political history. Uneducated teachers produce uneducated students.

Before this tussle between the old and the new history, historians used to be able to write for the people. Donald Creighton's biography of Macdonald is now outdated and it was written in prose that sounds florid today, but in the early 1950s his two volumes struck a chord with the literate public, who found themselves swept up in John A.'s efforts to create a nation out of fractious, far-flung colonies. Creighton's prose was stylish, if academic, but it could be read by anyone with interest in the subject—and there were tens of thousands of those.

But historians have since turned inward. Just as political scientists and economists have withdrawn from public dialogue, so too have most historians. Social and economic historians discourse learnedly about their cliometric methodologies, their number-crunching techniques and regression indices, and the past and present dialectical disputes that continue to exercise them. A few of the new history practitioners have turned themselves into advocates, preaching revolution like the Marxist labour historians, or calling for the rectification of past injustices for women or native peoples. But neither students nor general readers much care—all they know is that they can scarcely understand the graphs and equations or stilted and politically correct "prose" that lies on the page before them.

I have selected a few examples of poor writing, almost randomly chosen from recent economic and social history publications by Canadian historians:

We estimate univariate models of the price level and the exchange rate (data on Canadian interest rates are not available). We also estimate two multivariate models of the price level in which the independent variables are the U.S. price level and the money stock—variables which economic theory suggests would affect the price level. In each case, the impact of the formation of the bank is tested by an analysis of the stability of the regression and by an examination of the regression residuals.

The strategies railroad families adopted for survival and well-being revealed some striking continuities. Nevertheless, there were changes as well. Married women of the first generation provided for their families' welfare through their labour in the home. A number of second-generation wives, however, also contributed as secondary wage earners. During the Great Depression, running-trades families had to abandon temporarily their emphasis on occupational inheritance as a means of providing security for the next generation.

By helping to create categories of belonging and exclusion, nationalist histories are implicated in racism. Inevitability [*sic*] they affirm the continuities between the past and present of the nation for some, and are silent on the histories of others. . . . In this respect, nationalist histories contribute to the mythology that some people "naturally" belong in the country, while others are interlopers, "sojourners," or aliens. Insofar as they construct their narratives from the points of view of those who are inside the nation, they also obscure the complexity of people's lives (including imagined ones) between people within and without the nation's ideological boundaries.

It was the image of Aboriginal women as immoral and corrupting influences that predominated in the non-Aboriginal society that was taking shape. Authorities used this characterization to define and treat Aboriginal women, increasingly narrowing their options and opportunities. Both informal and formal constraints served to keep Aboriginal people from the towns and settled areas of the prairies and their presence there became more and more marginal. While they may not have wished to live in the towns, their land-use patterns for a time intersected with the new order and they might have taken advantage of markets and other economic opportunities.*

Why struggle through thickets of unreadable prose? Why not read that novel or turn on the TV?

Or why not pick up Pierre Berton's latest book of popular history and enjoy yourself for an hour or two? Berton moved into the terrain abandoned so foolishly by the academic historians, and he found broad, sweeping subjects that captured huge audiences. All were themes of national importance and national interest, and the professional historians had either abandoned them totally or written about them in such an abstruse form that only a few specialists had any interest in reading them. The field was open for Berton, Peter C. Newman, and a few dozen more journalists-turned-popular historians. They found intrinsic interest in the stories of the Canadian past and, as they learned how to do the archival research that historians had always done, they lost none of their skill with words. Their

---

70

*None of these examples is as impenetrable as that produced by the winners of the annual Bad Writing Contest sponsored by the scholarly journal *Philosophy and Literature*. One of this year's scholars offered this sentence: "If such a sublime cyborg would insinuate the future as post-Fordist subject, his palpably masochistic locations as ecstatic agent of the sublime superstate need to be decoded as the 'now-all-but-unreadable DNA' of a fast deindustrializing Detroit, just as his Robocop-like strategy of carceral negotiation and street control remains the tirelessly American one of inflicting regeneration through violence upon the racially heteroglossic wilds and others of the inner city."

stories leapt off the pages, captivating Canadians—and inform-
ing them. The best of the journalists became the nation's story-
tellers, the creators and keepers of the national mythos.

The response of professional academic historians to the
intruders was predictable. The absence of footnotes was decried,
the quality of the research was sneered at, and the book reviews
in the academic journals were almost always devastating. I have
written some reviews like this myself. Of course, academic journals almost always reviewed books a year or two after their
publication, so if you were Pierre Berton and your book had
already sold 100,000 copies in its first season, who cared? But on
the few occasions when the journalist-historians took on the
academics in debate, they usually did well, their command of
the subject every bit as impressive as that of the specialists. In the
Canadian Historical Review, Newman, for example, absolutely
savaged the historians who had attacked his treatment of native
women in his books on the Hudson's Bay Company.

I continue to believe that the nation's history is too important
to be left only to journalists. The writing of first-class history
about the national experience is something with which Canadian professional historians ought to be concerned. "The struggle for Canadian independence and the crises in national
survival," political scientist Daniel Drache wrote, are "the great
themes of Canadian history," but they do not move today's
historians. Most prefer to remain alone in their specialists'
cubbyholes, rather than to reach out to treat subjects that tell

Canadian students and citizens who they are, where they have come from, and where they are going.

In 1967 the president of the Canadian Historical Association, Richard Saunders, told his members that "a nation is a venture in history, that through an understanding of its history, it knows itself, finds confidence to be true to itself, and guidance for the future." Such words were overtly nationalist, as might have been expected in Centennial year. But such words would not often be uttered by any president thereafter; instead, it was Canadians' "limited identities," a phrase popularized in 1969 by historians Ramsay Cook and J.M.S. Careless, that would be preached and praised. Limited identities were almost openly anti-nationalist: it was not the nation that mattered, but "smaller, differentiated provincial or regional societies"; not Canadians as a whole, but the components of the ethnic mosaic; not Canadians as a society, but Canadians in their social classes. Canadians formed a complex pluralist society, and in that lay our strength.

The result of this perspective, as Michael Bliss put it in 1991, was the "sundering" of Canadian history, a sundering that mirrored the fragmentation of the nation. The result we live with every day is a separatist-minded Quebec, an unhappy West, and a Charter of Rights–driven emphasis on individual or group rights. The result for Canadian history, Bliss wrote, is the apparent triumph of studies "of pork-packing, Marxist labour organizers, social control in insane asylums . . . fourth-rate nineteenth century philosophers, parish politics, and, as J.L. Granatstein recently put it, 'the history of housemaid's knee in Belleville in the 1890s.' 'Really, who cares?' he also said." I did say that, and I have been denounced for it ever since. It was an overstatement, to be sure, but it reflected my increasing uneasiness and complete frustration at the way our history is taught.

Perhaps the story is not yet terminally bleak. There are still first-rate historians who produce books of large-scale narrative, on important national themes, that achieve popular appeal. John English's biography of Lester Pearson is a masterful work, Michael Bliss's studies of Banting and insulin are superb, and other scholars such as Desmond Morton, Doug Owram, Robert Bothwell, David Bercuson, and Terry Copp have combined sound scholarship and high-quality prose to break out of the academic historians' narrow confines. They have won substantial sales and good reviews, and they study the people every bit as much as the new-style historians do, though they fit them into a broader context than the current dominant cadre of practitioners. These scholars try to write about Canada as a nation, a people joined together by a rich history of great achievements and, yes, terrible failures. Their colleagues, however, remain distinctly unimpressed—if it's national history, if it's readable, and if it sells, it can't be any good. As three women historians in British Columbia said, the call for the restoration of "real" history "is implicitly a call to reinstate the history of great men, male politicians, and high politics to our educational system" rather than to meet feminists' demands "for a new history which includes the experiences of women, minorities and working people." It's not, but the struggle to try to persuade these advocates of any view of the past but their own is terribly wearing.

At the root of the social historians' response is envy. The academic historians who retain an interest in national history are regularly called on as commentators on radio and television; the specialists are not, and this disparity in public attention even led a panel at a meeting of the Canadian Historical Association to bewail the unfairness of it all. These critics do not seem to realize that the national historians have something to say that viewers and listeners want to hear. Moreover, the "academic readable" historians sell books in their thousands (the journalist popular historians sell in the tens of thousands) and actually earn some money from their writing. The "academic unreadable" historians sell not at all and earn scarcely a penny. The standard university press run for most specialized academic history books is now about 400 to 800 copies, usually tending toward the lower end. Royalties, if they are paid at all, are in the range of 1 to 5 percent of the net price, compared with 10 to 15 percent of the list price paid by trade publishers. The price of academic books is inevitably high—usually above $40—and their only destination is university libraries. Even the specialists no longer buy the books published by their peers; certainly the public does not purchase them. At least public money no longer goes to support the Aid to Scholarly Publication program with subsidies that ran upwards of $7000 a volume.

The vast majority of scholarly books are destined to remain unread on university library shelves. How long the university presses, which operate with the assistance of public funds, can keep on printing such dogs is unclear; if the subsidies disappear, as they probably will, these scholarly publishers will have to adapt or die. Whether academic writers can change enough to reach readers, whether they even want to, is uncertain.

The point is not that scholarly publishing is unnecessary. It is vitally necessary that research into our past and present be undertaken in the universities. However, one may legitimately question the use of public funds to publish books whose only true value is to secure tenure or promotion in the universities for the authors. The unreadable sludge could be circulated to the three interested readers in *samizdat* form or made available on the Internet. To secure a subsidy, I believe a book must be able to be read and understood by those who put up the cash.

Unfortunately, the scholarly journals are, if anything, even worse than the scholarly books. In a recent editorial in *Saturday Night* (May 1997), editor Kenneth Whyte had a field day poking fun at the *Canadian Historical Review*, the premier journal in the field of Canadian history, and one I was the editor of more than a decade ago: "Articles in the journal are long and turgid, as limited in scope as they are timid in judgment and questionable in relevance. The book reviews are not reviews so much as what in elementary school we called book reports—mere summaries of the contents, written without wit or reflection. Rigorous criticisms are rare, though in the current issue a scholar reviewing a text on railway regulation does puff himself up and argue definitively that "a sentence at the bottom of page 22 should have a 'not' in it." Whyte was right. The scholarly historians have let down the side, totally and completely, and there is no sign that the trend toward academic obfuscation will soon be reversed.

Now, it may only be a coincidence that the turn away from national and political history took place at the same time that Canada began to fragment. Did the historians' shift to victimization and blame-seeking on the fringes, to a peoples' history, and to abstract, abstruse language lead Canada's plunge toward dissolution, or did it merely reflect what was happening in the body politic? I admit this is a chicken-and-egg question without any credible answer, but national historians of the future—if there are any and if there is still a nation—may well be fascinated by the way the trends came together. Tragically, at a time when it was critical that Canadians understand their political and constitutional history, historians wanted to talk tiny, trivial subjects of little or no general interest.

Where do we go from here? Doug Owram, one of the best of the newer generation of Canadian historians and a scholar with fine credentials in social and intellectual history, put it clearly. None of the new approaches and new theses, he wrote, have yet to achieve widespread acceptance among Canadian historians; "none can even be said to have reached the level where we can talk about a school of interpretation." Why? Perhaps it is because this nation, "so supposedly fragmented and 'limited,' has had a common historical experience of considerable duration, living under common laws, social programs, and with cultural and social ties that have national as well as local characteristics." Perhaps, Owram argued, the time has come to look at the national experience again, at "the interplay between those identities and the way in which that particular complex and dynamic interplay distinguishes this country from the rest of the world . . . The current generation of historians has shied away from any attempt at overarching interpretive frameworks. Perhaps the time has come for them to think consciously about the issue." In other words, to think of Canada as a nation, as a whole, as a society, and not simply as a collection of races, genders, regions, and classes.

The trend away from the particular in Canada has been slow to take form—far too slow. But in Britain, the United States, and Europe, national history is again starting to take its proper place. Scholars and newspaper columnists, politicians and popular historians argue about the importance of the past, shout abuse at their opponents, and generally act as if the national history and the way it is written and taught matters. It does matter—except in Canada, where the historical amnesia is all but terminal and where Canadian history as a profession is once again as backward as it was a quarter-century ago when the labour historians started the revolution against their seniors.

"Of only one thing we may be certain," Carl Berger wrote in *The Writing of Canadian History*, "in time the new history will experience the same fate as the old history." Clio, the muse of history, he noted, "has the alarming habit of devouring those who respond to her charms." I believe that the pendulum will swing, and the new debate will eventually happen in Canada, too. And not too soon for those who believe that Sir Wilfrid Laurier was right when he said that the twentieth century belonged to Canada. The Canadian experiment, for all our current preoccupations, has been one of success, not failure.

CHAPTER 4

Multicultural Mania

In July 1996, the holder of the chair in Sikh Studies at the University of British Columbia gave up his position. Professor Harjot Oberoi, a Punjabi-born scholar who had held the chair since its establishment in 1987, was for all practical purposes driven from it. The reason was simple: his book on Sikh history, *The Construction of Religious Boundaries*, published by a prestigious university press, had argued that Sikhism had its roots in Hinduism and Islam. But local Sikh religious and community leaders were outraged—the Sikh faith, they believe, is both divinely inspired and completely separate from Hinduism.

A minor squabble between fundamentalists and scholars? Of course, but one with greater significance. The UBC chair in Sikh Studies was one of many chairs established at Canadian universities under the aegis of the federal government's multiculturalism program. The UBC chair had been created with $350,000 raised from within the Sikh community and a matching grant provided by Ottawa. In other words, Canadians' tax dollars had been used to establish the post, and the outrage of a small section of the tax-paying community had been used to drive Oberoi from it.

This sad story has equivalents elsewhere. The Sikh Studies program at the University of Toronto was discontinued in the early 1990s after similar protests from fundamentalists who objected to what was being taught; the Ukrainian Studies chair at the same university, again heavily supported by federal funds, was long a focus of controversy in the 1980s; and similar tales can be told of other ethnic studies' chairs in many Canadian universities. Jewish Canadians want their story told in ways that are acceptable to the community, and so do German, Chinese, Japanese, and black Canadians, among others.

So what? Every ethnic group, every religion, has an idealized version of its past. And there is nothing wrong with that. As York University political scientist Reg Whitaker put it, without the politically correct cant that dominates debate in Canada, "If religious groups want to offer money to universities for chairs in 'studies' that will prohibit genuine scholarship in favour of religious dogma, they are of course free to do so." However, any university "that wishes to retain a scholarly reputation would be advised to steer well clear of any such fool's gold." But at the University of British Columbia, Whitaker concluded, the Sikh Studies chair was endowed by both community money and taxpayers' money. "With Dr Oberoi, we may have received value for money, but now the 'community' . . . has exercised a *de facto* veto placing faith ahead of scholarship . . . Multicultural mumbo jumbo aside, governments have no business throwing tax dollars into efforts by religious or cultural minorities to preen their own self-images. They can do that on their own." But Canadian governments—federal, provincial, and municipal—have been throwing money for years into multicultural education and, in the process, the history of Canada, where it is even taught, has been distorted out of all recognition. Guilt, victimhood, redress, and the avoidance of offence—those are the watchwords that rule today.

It ought not to be necessary to put what follows in personal terms, but racism can be a damaging charge, and it is one that Canadians throw about very loosely these days.

I am the child of immigrants. My grandparents on my mother's side and my father escaped from a hostile, intolerant Europe and made their difficult way to Canada. Here they made new lives for themselves and their offspring, and here they slowly adapted themselves to a new culture in a new land. They suffered from racial prejudice and religious mistrust, and there was no one to tell them how the country and its government worked. Yet, they gradually (and perhaps to their surprise) found themselves becoming Canadians, attached to this best of all possible lands and part of its present and future. I was born and educated here, and I too am attached to Canada, very much so. It has been, is, and will always remain God's Country to me and mine.

As the child of immigrants, I cannot in conscience be against immigration. The glory of this nation is that its people, including even its native people, came from somewhere else. I want this epic adventure to continue, and I believe that most Canadians, however much they fret about being overrun or worry about the numbers who flood into this country in hard economic times, take substantial pride in having their nation keep its doors open to the world. The race, religion, and colour bars of the past are long gone, and good riddance to them. This does not mean that Canada should exercise no controls over those who seek to come here—any country has the right and the duty to determine whom it admits—but I believe our policy toward immigrants and refugees should be as liberal as economic conditions permit. My primary concern, therefore, is not who comes to Canada, and not even how many come here.

What worries me is what happens to immigrants and refugees *after* they arrive on our shores. How do the Canadian people react to them? How does the state deal with them? How does it teach their children and how does it acculturate them to Canadian society? How does it prepare them to become responsible citizens with an understanding of Canada's culture, society, laws, and government?

Does the nation tell newcomers that because they have come to a formed society they must accept its ways and adapt to its norms, including academic freedom within the universities? I believe it should. Does it tell immigrants that they must leave their Old World political baggage at the water's edge? I believe it should. Does it say to newcomers that while they may keep as much of their native culture as they wish, they must pay the costs involved? I believe it should.

The aim of every Canadian and of all levels of government should be to welcome immigrants and to turn them into Canadian citizens as quickly as possible by giving them the cultural knowledge they need to understand and to thrive in our society. If immigrants feel the need to associate with others like themselves and to maintain their ties to the Old Country, more power to them. But they and their communities must accept that, in Canada, political opponents and people with cultural and religious differences do not kill each other or try to censor others into silence. They must also come to understand that if they wish to honour the Old Country's ways and practices, they must do it themselves. They should pay for language and heritage instruction on their own, and not one cent of federal, provincial, or municipal government money should be devoted to fostering the retention of their cultures.

The state should spend its limited funds on helping newcomers to adapt to Canadian society by teaching them the basic knowledge, the symbols, and the ideas that literate, culturally aware Canadians understand and use to communicate with each other. To do anything else condemns immigrants to isolation, to

85

low-paying jobs, to the expanding ghetto of the ill-paid and uneducated. Instead of practising what the Toronto Board of Education does—grafting multicultural content onto all subject areas—the schools should teach more about Canada, something that might actually be of use to the students. Teach immigrants and their children to read and speak the country's official languages; train them in the requirements of Canadian citizenship and, where necessary, explain how a democracy functions; instruct them, especially their offspring, in Canada's history and in the roots of our nationhood; give them the cultural capital that literate and aware Canadians share. Make them good Canadians, in other words. Do not turn immigrants loose to fend for themselves, to struggle alone to master the strange ways of a new and bewilderingly complex society. Do not tell them, do not even imply, that they can stay East Indian, Somali, Jamaican, German, Chinese, or Chilean and succeed in Canada. Their children might integrate and do well, simply because of the enormous assimilative powers of North American society, but the first generation, if they choose to remain apart, cannot.

I believe that current multiculturalism policies and use of government funds promote such separateness. This is not only a shameless waste of tax dollars—one undertaken for partisan political, not national, advantage—but a terrible squandering of human resources. Even worse, the policies of multiculturalism have created the idea among immigrants (and even among native-born citizens, especially in francophone Quebec) that Canada, and in particular English-speaking Canada, has no culture and no nationality of its own. If it did, they ask with some justification, why would the government not try to show it to them? Why else would it fund newcomers to preserve their old ways?

Canadians, of course, would have to agree on just what their national identity is and how best to pass it on to immigrants. For example, they have always denied that Canada is a melting pot like the United States. Here, in the Canadian mosaic, the claim goes, there was no imposed conformity, no national mythology, no effort to blend all together. I think this mosaic is a myth and that Canada was every bit as much a melting pot as the United States. Immigrants came to the dominion in the nineteenth and twentieth centuries, learned English or French, went to school and sang "Rule Britannia" and "The Maple Leaf Forever"* until the 1950s and "O Canada" after that. They

---

*Not any more. A perfect small example of political correctness occurred in the summer of 1997 when two recent immigrants from Romania and the United States combined to "modernize" the words to "The Maple Leaf Forever." That old anthem, little sung today, had been the favourite of my generation of schoolchildren because of its deathless words, "Wolfe the donk-less hero came"—or so we always sang it. But the new version, hailing Canada's "emerald fields," was politically correct in every respect. One letter writer to the *Globe and Mail* (25 June 1997) made the obvious point: if "The Maple Leaf Forever" could be altered, so should the French-language version of "O Canada," whose words, "Il sait porter la croix," were "highly offensive and inappropriate in the multicultural context in which we live." Another writer, with equal bitterness, demanded satirically (I think) that "God Save the Queen" be changed to refer neither to a deity nor to a gender-specific monarch. Oh, Canada!

participated in school Christmas pageants, they read from the same texts, and they listened to the same radio programs or watched the same TV. Italian, Ukrainian, Chinese, and British immigrants alike became union members, and hockey and baseball players, and men and women who volunteered to fight for their country in the First and Second World Wars and in Korea. For some reason, perhaps because we were looking for ways to differentiate ourselves from the United States, or perhaps because of our different history, Canadians pretended that there was no melting pot here. There was—though it differed in some important ways from that south of the border.

Canada certainly lacked a unifying nationalist myth that bound the country together. Though some historians argued that "Canada's nationhood was born on Vimy Ridge," they forgot that there was only a single regiment of Québécois in the Canadian Corps and that more than half the Canadian soldiers in that battle in 1917 had immigrated from Britain. It might have been more correct to say that *English-Canadian* nationalism was born on Vimy Ridge. The simple, if regrettable, truth was that French- and English-speaking Canadians had differing interpretations of the country's past, present, and future. Moreover, the colonial link to Britain meant that British monarchs and governors general, not Canadian leaders, sat at the top of the greasy pole. North American life absorbed those who came here, to be sure, but the psychic unifying force of North Americanism was substantially weaker in its Canadian variant.

There is another telling difference between the two North American societies. In the United States, major public figures have spoken out against multiculturalism and what they see as its potentially baneful effects. Arthur Schlesinger, the distinguished American historian with gilt-edged liberal Democratic credentials, wrote in *The Disuniting of America*:

> *E pluribus unum.* The United States had a brilliant solution for the inherent fragility of a multiethnic society: the creation of a brand-new national identity, carried forward by individuals who, in forsaking old loyalties and joining to make new lives, melted away ethnic differences. Those intrepid Europeans . . . *wanted* to forget a horrid past and to embrace a hopeful future. They *expected* to become Americans. . . . The point of America was not to preserve old cultures, but to forge a new *American* culture.

Idealized view though this may have been, it was far better than what now exists. "The new ethnic gospel," Schlesinger complained,

> rejects the unifying vision of individuals from all nations melted into a new race. Its underlying philosophy is that America is not a nation of individuals at all but a nation of groups, that ethnicity is the defining

experience for most Americans, that ethnic ties are permanent and indelible, and that division into ethnic communities establishes the basic structure of American society and the basic meaning of American history.

This is terribly dangerous, Schlesinger argues, because it threatens to dissolve the glue that holds the United States together. No longer is America a society of individuals making their own choices. America is becoming a society of groups fixed in their ethnic character.

Schlesinger is not alone among the intellectual heavyweights opposing multiculturalism. Robert Hughes, the iconoclastic Australian who has lived in the United States since 1970 and who is well known for his art criticism in *Time*, focused in his book, *Culture of Complaint: The Fraying of America*, on what he calls "multi-culti and its discontents." He equates multiculturalism—an idea that suggests implicitly that people can live together—with the new separatism that he, like Schlesinger, sees engulfing America. He savagely belittles "Eurocentrism," the charge that higher education is dominated by the writings and ideas of dead white males. "Unhappily you do not have to listen very long . . . before sensing that, in quite a few of its proponents' minds, multiculturalism means something less than genuine curiosity about other cultural forms." To Hughes, multiculturalism means separatism, the disastrous cutting of the ties that bind America—and Western thought—together.

So disturbing has the rise of multicultural pressures become that Richard Rorty, a distinguished academic, felt compelled to argue in the *New York Times* in early 1994 that *Americans* need a national identity. Rorty denounced the proponents of multiculturalism as "unpatriotic" because they repudiated the idea of a national identity and the emotion of national pride. It is important, he argued, "to insist that a sense of shared national identity is not an evil. It is an absolutely essential component of citizenship, of any attempt to take our country and its problems seriously. There is no incompatibility between respect for cultural differences and American patriotism."

Schlesinger, Hughes, and Rorty have seen the future, and they know it will not work. Schlesinger looked briefly at Canada in his book on disuniting America and pronounced this country "vulnerable to schism" because Canada, unlike the United States, lacks a unique national identity. Canadians, unlike Americans, have never developed "a strong sense of what it means to be a Canadian"; instead, and wrongly, they "inclined for generous reasons to a policy of official multiculturalism."

The one certainty is that the ideal of the American melting pot *as it now exists* is no model for Canada. The polity in the United States is in the process of breaking down. If Canadians want a melting pot, they will have to hark back to an earlier version of America. If they want to meld immigrants and ethnic groups into Canadian society, they will have to ensure that they have unifying ideas and symbols for newcomers to hold onto. In the United States of the 1900s and the 1940s, such ideas and symbols were omnipresent. In Canada, since the demise of the British connection, and especially since the advent of multiculturalism as government policy, such ideas and symbols never have been, and we pay the price for that now.

In October 1996, Heritage Canada released a report on multiculturalism that found much public dissatisfaction with the concept. There is, the government was told unmistakably, a backlash from vast numbers of conservative-minded Canadians who see multiculturalism as divisive, and who fear for social cohesion in light of the demands of ethnic and linguistic groups. So, to policy makers in Ottawa, what was the best way to counter these perceptions? Not to integrate newcomers; not to teach recent arrivals in Canada about the heritage of the country to which they have come. No, the key point was that the government should promote a "new" Canadian identity based on justice, peace, and "compassionate solidarity" rather than on history and geographical considerations! As Liberal multiculturalism minister Hedy Fry said, multiculturalism is about "the core Canadian values of fairness and respect, compassion and equality," about building bridges between communities and individuals of all backgrounds.

In other words, more bafflegab. The federal government, the provinces, and the school boards simply fail to realize that the backlash against multiculturalism comes from the widespread realization that it will erode the history and the heritage that

Canadians share. Canadians want justice, peace, and compassionate solidarity, to be sure, but they also instinctively believe that they have their own history and heritage. They see no reason why it should be eliminated by government fiat for a misguided policy that tries to make everyone feel good. As the teachers at one high school said, the pressure is on to teach everyone's history but our own. And so it has been for the quarter-century since the Trudeau government endorsed multiculturalism as an official policy in 1971. A decade later, the Canadian Charter of Rights and Freedoms entrenched multiculturalism in the Constitution, and, in 1987, the Canadian Multiculturalism Act expanded the concept further still. Entrenched in this way, bolstered by federal, provincial, and municipal funds, multiculturalism is an article of faith for politicians of all stripes and for educators. It must be defended and protected, and whatever threatens it must be rooted out—even if that threat is the teaching of Canadian history.

There is racism in Canadian society now, and there has been in the past. But Canada has never had the brutal, murderous race riots that have so disfigured American society. Our citizenship is open to everyone who lives here for three years and who qualifies, in contrast to many European nations that have a citizenship of "blood." Yet, Canadians try to demonstrate to themselves and the world that we are a deeply racist society. The past must be destroyed *in toto* so that we can build anew the perfect multicultural society with the new "core Canadian values" predominant.

What do we teach children? That the Indians were the victims of white genocide and, more recently, the white appropriation of their voice.* That immigrants were shamefully maltreated by Canadians and, in Quebec, that Québécois have been repeatedly humiliated by the Anglo majority that tried to assimilate them and make them fight in British wars. That blameless Ukrainian Canadians, Italian Canadians, and Japanese Canadians were interned by the federal government during the two world wars. That Canada was anti-Semitic and turned away the Jews of Europe fleeing Hitler. That blacks have been persecuted in Canada.**

Much of this is true, but in history, context is all-important. Consider the internment of Ukrainians during the Great War, for example. Ukrainians in substantial numbers lived in the old country under the rule of the Austro-Hungarian Empire, a country with which the British Empire, including Canada, went to war in August 1914. The senior Ukrainian bishop in Canada at

---

* On January 7, 1998, just before this book went to press, the federal government apologized to Aboriginal Canadians for "the role it played in the development and administration of Indian residential schools. At the same time, it pledged to "look for ways of . . . reflecting Louis Riel's proper place in history." The first apology might be justifiable; it is certainly politically expedient. The second promise is not something a government can or should attempt—the past cannot be altered by government fiat.

** In an interview, one high school teacher argued that "we make Canada look very positive . . . we paint a rosy picture [but] Canada has some black marks against it and texts don't reflect this." It is difficult to imagine how many more "black marks" could be squeezed into the curriculum. And why should any nation's texts stress the "black marks"?

the outbreak of war urged his compatriots to be loyal to their emperor, Franz Joseph, an astonishingly ignorant and unthinking act that led to much hardship, especially for immigrants who had come to Canada for a new life in a country free of Old World hatreds. What was Ottawa to do? In a war, in a nation that was ordinarily suspicious of foreigners and especially so of "enemy aliens," fear ran rampant, and harmless Ukrainians were public scapegoats for an enemy that could not be reached. There were mistakes and stupidities aplenty in the locking up of many ordinary men in work camps, but this was not genocide. This reaction was legitimate under Canadian law and the law of war, and there is no case for financial compensation or apology. The only apology owed, in fact, was that from the bishop to his flock.

That is not how these events are presented in Canada. Ukrainian-Canadian historians and activists have campaigned skilfully for redress, for the erection of plaques to commemorate the internment of their grandfathers, and for changes in the way history is taught. To some extent, they have succeeded.

The same story can be told about Italian Canadians in the Second World War. In the 1930s, Italy's consulates in Toronto and Montreal were active hotbeds of Fascism, soliciting support and dispensing propaganda for Mussolini's regime. During the Italo-Ethiopian War, an act of naked Italian aggression that began in 1935, money was raised for the war effort, including wedding rings donated by patriotic women. There was nothing wrong with this response—until Italy declared war against

Britain and France, and hence Canada, in June 1940. Then the Fascist connections of Italian-Canadian community leaders became, not useful demonstrations of social status, but a threat to Canadian security. Many were locked up behind barbed wire at Petawawa, Ontario; and they ought to have been. They were political and financial supporters of an odious authoritarian regime with which Canada was at war, and, while they were entitled to fair treatment, they were not entitled to sympathy. Too many mistakes were made by an inefficient RCMP, and those who were wrongly sent away were owed compensation. Italian Canadians, emboldened by the success of other groups and by a sympathetic National Film Board documentary that distorted history shamefully, tried for a blanket apology and financial redress to all. They are simply not entitled to it.

Then there are the Japanese Canadians, the one group that did receive both an apology and financial compensation from Brian Mulroney's Progressive Conservative government. In the public mind today, the Japanese Canadians of 1941, all 22,000 of them, were interned after the outbreak of war in the Pacific on 7 December 1941, for no reason other than their racial origin. The Liberal government of Mackenzie King acted out of racist motives, nothing more. This received version is both right and wrong. There is no doubt that the vast majority of Japanese Canadians posed no threat to anyone. But the Japanese consul-general in Vancouver was actively propagandizing and prosely-tizing among his fellow and former countrymen (all of whom were citizens under Japanese law and in Tokyo's eyes), and he was under orders to recruit spies. Incriminating telegrams directing such activities were decoded by Washington and were known to Ottawa. There was also near-panic in British Columbia as the Japanese swept across the Pacific, and both the provincial government and "vigilante" groups were demanding action. In February 1942 Ottawa gave in to the pressures and ordered the evacuation—not internment—of Japanese Canadians from the coast to the interior. Some 700 Japanese Canadians were interned at Angler in northern Ontario, but these men were deemed threats to Canadian security or were self-declared supporters of the Japanese Empire.

This rough justice ruined lives and destroyed many Japanese Canadians financially. But there was a war on, there was a real fear of attack and even invasion, and Japanese fifth-columnists had already demonstrated how devastatingly effective they could be throughout Asia. At the least, Ottawa's actions can be defended as militarily necessary. What cannot be justified was the judicial theft of Japanese-Canadian property, a shameful event in Canadian history; thousands scrambled to pick up the belongings of the evacuees for a song. For this loss, Japanese Canadians were justly entitled to compensation. For the evacuation, no apology was needed. Even democracies have the right to defend themselves. In early 1942, with the war going very badly, Ottawa, its military commanders on the Pacific, the government in Victoria, and the overwhelming majority of the

British Columbia population believed Canada had to act. As it turned out, there was no attack on the west coast, aside from a single submarine shelling the Estevan Point lighthouse—but no one knew this in February 1942.

The postwar Japanese-Canadian community lobbied long and hard for redress and finally won it. I believe the Mulroney government's action was half right, but governments should not try to alter history's decisions. If they do, they owe the past the courtesy of explaining why decisions were made. In the climate of the 1980s, in the atmosphere of multiculturalism, victimhood, and guilt, no such explanations were offered. Canadians were told only that their forebears had acted brutally in a racialist way, that there was no military threat and no danger of espionage, and that internment was completely unjustified. Well, yes and no.

So strong was the desire among good liberal-minded Canadians to embrace guilt that anyone who questioned the apology and redress to Japanese Canadians was *de facto* a bigot. When I wrote a *Saturday Night* article on the history behind the issue and published a subsequent book (with Masako Iino and Hiroko Takamura, two Japanese historians, and Patricia Roy, a British Columbia historian), I was subjected to the worst barracking I have ever received. I was as racist as was the government in 1942, my facts were incorrect, and surely I could see that the government's interning of Japanese Canadians on purely racial grounds was the moral equivalent of the Holocaust. No, it wasn't—not even close. In the context of 1942, there was reason to fear the

98

loyalty of British Columbia Japanese, there was reason to believe that Japan had agents at work, and there was reason to believe that the Canadian army might have difficulty protecting Japanese Canadians against the attacks of other Canadians. All these statements are defensible, soundly based on evidence, and all but irrefutable. But they clashed with the culture of victimization and the desire of many Canadians to believe that they were just as guilty of racial sins as was any Nazi.

The Mulroney redress precedent, of course, emboldened every other ethnic group. As Columbia University historian Alan Brinkley said of the United States, where the mania for apologies is as widespread as in Canada:

> There are occasions when a government has been complicit in the commission of some grand wrong, the obscuring of it or both. And in those cases, an apology might be appropriate. It would, for instance, be a great thing for the Turkish government to apologize for the massacre of the Armenians—even though they were not the government in power then—because it continues to be officially denied. But, as a rule, if government is going to apologize, it should be for something it did rather than something that happened 100 years ago. And even then the consequences may well be perverse, opening the door to all kinds of frivolous demands and unresolvable controversies.

Brinkley was right. After the Japanese Canadians secured their redress, diverse other groups pressed their cases for apologies for the sins of past policy from which they had suffered. Undoubtedly, thousands were treated shamefully throughout history, from the deportation of the Acadians, to the head tax on the Chinese, to the immigration department's turning away of Jewish refugees, to discrimination against present-day Somalis in Toronto. But apologies and victimhood do not make for either good current policy or a proper collective understanding of history. Instead, they create cynicism in the majority of Canadians who feel that certain groups are trying to rip off public funds.

We all are aware that Canadians have sometimes acted shamefully. But Canadians in their 500 years in this most favoured of lands have committed relatively few atrocities when compared with virtually any other society. There are no Bosnian massacres in our past, no Armenian genocides, no Christian crusades or Muslim jihads. Canadians have fought and argued, cheated and stolen land, hated and feared, but ordinarily they have done so in relatively contained and constrained ways. We should know about the appalling episodes in our past, and we should try to learn from them. But to pretend that Canada has been and remains a monstrous regime with blood-stained hands, to suggest that Canadian history is one of brutal expropriation, genocidal behaviour, and rampant racism, simply does not wash.

Tell that to the public schools and high schools. Ontario's appalling 1993 *Guidelines for Ethnocultural Equity in School*

Boards complain that "Ontario's school system has been and continues to be mainly European in perspective. The prevalence of one cultural tradition limits students' opportunities to benefit from the contributions of people from a variety of backgrounds." The guidelines go on to say that "exclusion of the experiences, values, and viewpoints of Aboriginal and racial and ethnocultural minority groups constitutes a systemic barrier to success for students from those groups and often produces inequitable outcomes for them." The government's *Resource Guide for Antiracist and Ethnocultural Equity Education* (1992) makes the point that the province's schools, because they have been western European in content and perspective, have left students of other backgrounds believing that they have not been "represented in Canadian history" or not "represented positively. This failure of the system to give equal attention and respect to all groups has contributed to stereotyping." In other words, sugar-coat everything that is not positive for every non-white group and for immigrants other than those from northern Europe. On one level, the impact of such policy is that schools no longer feel able to celebrate a holiday such as Christmas unless they do the same for Muslim, Jewish, and Buddhist festivals. This reaction, silly though it be, drastically shortchanges all Canadians. Our civilization and culture *is* Western, and there is no reason we should be ashamed of it or not wish to teach our students about it. Canadians are the inheritors of Greek and Roman traditions and the British and French experience, and the West is the dominant civilization in the world today in part because its values have been tested and found true. To pretend that a simple relativism should apply in the schools and that immigrants, who have come here because they want to buy into our civilization and value system, should be told to retain their own culture is wrongheaded in the extreme. It also discriminates against newcomers by systemically patronizing and marginalizing them.

If only the rest of our history were taught and the racist interludes were presented in context, one might barely tolerate this perversion of fact. But it is not. To present university students with an article on the Japanese Canadians and to pretend that this one slice covers the national experience of the Second World War is a grotesque distortion, a complete absence of context. To use this same example in a public or high school history class with students who know nothing about the war, including which side Canada was on, is even worse. Yet, if presented with it in context, students in high school and in university could benefit from this lesson: how a war fought against Nazi racialist beliefs was marred by Canadian racism.

What this multicultural and antiracism emphasis on grievances has done is to reduce history to "a treasure-trove of incidents and examples which were used only to illuminate some present concern." Often, wrote Ken Osborne, a student of the school history curricula, "history disappeared as a course, to be replaced by a kind of mini-anthropology of Canada's constituent cultures. Multiculturalism painted Canada as a community of

102

communities, but its emphasis was on the plural rather than the singular . . . the final result was usually a series of discrete but mutually isolated heritages, united only by being located in the same political unit."

Let me be very clear: I do not want children to be taught an airbrushed history of Canada with all the warts removed. I do not want the experiences and contributions of non-Western cultures to be banned from the schools. Nor do I want a curriculum that is relentlessly political history, one that focuses on the "great men." What I want is what the schools and the nation need: a history that puts Canada up front, that points to the successes and failures of our past policies, and that gives due weight to the contributions made by non-charter-group Canadians. I want a history that puts Canada firmly in the context of Western civilization, but gives full weight to the non-Western world. I want a history that recognizes what men and women, great and ordinary, did to build a successful nation.

Sometimes the pursuit of political correctness becomes ridiculous. The statue of Samuel de Champlain on Nepean Point overlooking the Ottawa River in the nation's capital, for example, was denounced for its presentation of native Canadians. Champlain stood proudly atop the plinth, while below him knelt a native. It mattered not at all that the statue was a hundred years old. In the eyes of organized native groups, it was demeaning, and the figure of the Indian was soon removed. There was no unanimity among native leaders, however. One from the Rama First Nation band said: "What we would like to do is use the statue and learn from it. . . . Removing the figures and storing them in a warehouse . . . doesn't make sense. Isn't that what they did to Indians in the first place?"

Or consider the brief rediscovery of Clara Brett Martin. The first female lawyer in Canada and Ontario, she persevered against gender discrimination and was called to the Bar in 1897. Feminist legal historian Constance Backhouse, a writer who consciously set out to create feminist heroines, declared her an archetype, and soon universities named lecture series and research centres after her, and the Ontario government dubbed its attorney-general's main office building in her honour. All well and good, except that a diligent legal researcher discovered that Martin was anti-Semitic in her attitudes and actions as a Toronto property owner, and Robert Martin, a legal columnist and law professor at the University of Western Ontario, publicized the story. Poor Clara, so recently rediscovered, was interred again in ignominy. Again, historical context was totally absent. In the early twentieth century, anti-Semitism was common, indeed accepted, in Canada, the United States, Britain, and Western Europe. It was not right, but it was present, and Martin was simply a woman of her era, though one more courageous and determined than most of her peers. Political correctness had motivated her sanctification, and political correctness led to her subsequent demonization. Those who are brought to life again

104

only because of the abuse and misreading of history apparently are doomed once more to perish by it.

My point is, or should be, simple: history happened. The object is not to undo it, distort it, or to make it fit our present political attitudes. The object of history, which each generation properly interprets anew, is to understand what happened and why. A multicultural Canada can and should look at its past with fresh eyes. It should, for example, study how the Ukrainians came to Canada, how they were treated, how they lived, sometimes suffered, ultimately prospered, and became Canadians. What historians should not do is to recreate history to make it serve present purposes. They should not obscure or reshape events to make them fit political agendas. They should not declare whole areas of the past off-limits because they can only be presented in politically unfashionable terms any more than they should fail to draw object lessons from a past that was frequently less than pleasant and less than honourable.

Because the past was not perfect, it must not be made perfect today. Yes, students should not be exposed to prejudicial references in their texts. It does no one any good to refer to Indians as savages (though that was how their white contemporaries described them from the sixteenth century on), or to teach gender inequality and racial superiority. But our past is littered with these usages, and the danger exists—and, as we have seen, it is very real—that a worthy present requirement can quickly begin to distort what happened in the past. And so it has. "We can become so afraid of offending anyone," said McMaster University historian John Trueman, "that we end up satisfying no one." The result is that "history as we have known it and taught it will simply cease to exist in the schools."

Not only were school curricula to be swept clean of any "offensive" materials but the actual learning environment was to be monitored. In Ontario, for example, Bob Rae's NDP government, the most perfectly Politically Correct government in Canadian history, adopted a policy of "zero tolerance" of discrimination and harassment in the universities. The successor Harris government has not declared the policy inoperative. Students and faculty are to be protected against discrimination because of race, creed, sex, sexual orientation, disability, age, dialect, and accent. Harassment is defined as "something that is known or might reasonably be known to be offensive, hostile, and inappropriate." Another offence is the creation of a "negative environment," and "a complainant does not have to be a direct target to be adversely affected by a negative environment."

The impact of such a policy on a university classroom should be obvious. If I were a student of German origin in a course studying the Holocaust, could I not reasonably feel the victim of a negative environment? An Iraqi-born student in a class on the present Middle East? A Chinese immigrant in a class on the Korean War? Or a Québécois in a class studying federalism? How easy it could be to make a student feel marginalized, excluded, harassed, the victim of a negative environment. That students might learn from having inherent prejudices challenged did not occur to the Rae government.

If this hostile approach to untrammelled learning existed and still exists in the universities, how much stronger was it in the public and high schools of Ontario? The Toronto Board of Education in 1994 produced a policy statement on "racial and ethnocultural mistreatment" that defined a negative environment as the product of "acts or omissions that maintain offensive, hostile or intimidating climates for study or work for individuals or groups." Such an environment was "characterized by inappropriate choices in, or lack of attention to, a racially and culturally inclusive and equitable curriculum and pedagogy." In other words, every teacher was on notice to be very careful that course content did not upset students and their parents. There would be no "stereotyping and bias in curriculum and pedagogy," no "historical and factual misrepresentations." If only one ethnic group's facts were the same as another's. Of course, they are not.

Ontario is the clearest example of this trend in Canada, but the other provinces in their own disparate ways are moving in the same direction. All attempt to remove anything offensive, for whatever reason, from school curricula and learning materials, and all commit themselves to introduce positive materials about minorities, their cultures, and their past, present, and future contributions to the nation. All work to train teachers and principals, and, as one federally financed course offered in

Toronto put it, "to reduce principal and teacher resistance to multicultural and anti-racist education."

Because our own history has been so neglected, inevitably American culture, carried by TV, movies, magazines, and clothes, sweeps all before it. Walt Disney is the cultural norm for students, the master of past and present, and Bart Simpson the exemplar. Canadian students probably know more American history than about Canadian. As political scientist Gad Horowitz lamented the passing of Canada: "Multiculturalism is the masochistic celebration of Canadian nothingness."

CHAPTER 5

No Flanders Fields? Canadians, War, and Remembrance

I had the opportunity of attending the fiftieth anniversary celebrations of D-Day in Normandy and London in June 1994, and the fiftieth anniversary commemoration of V-E Day in Apeldoorn and London in May 1995 with the Canadian Broadcasting Corporation. These were astonishing, wrenchingly emotional events that left me and many of those who participated in them in tears much of the time. To watch the old men, once young, march through the streets of Courseulles, St. Aubin, and Apeldoorn, Amsterdam, Groningen, and fifty small Dutch towns was to realize how quickly time passes, how soon we are old. The two commemorative events also made many Canadians aware again how little, in contrast to Western Europeans, Canadians know of what their soldiers did a half-century ago.

The Dutch certainly know of the First Canadian Army. In May 1995 in the Netherlands, the one country in the world where Canadians are universally hailed as liberators, every house was decorated in the colours of the House of Orange and with Canadian flags. Home-made banners, obviously erected by ordinary citizens or neighbourhood associations and not by the state or municipalities, seemed to stretch across every street. I especially remember the theme of gratitude, written in English on one banner in Apeldoorn, that was clear to all: "Bless You, Boys."

The Dutch remember the war. They remember the brutality of the Nazi occupation, the starvation winter of 1944–45, the executions of resistance fighters that went on into May 1945, and the collaboration of many of their men and women with the oppressors. They remember, but they no longer hate the Germans, with whom they willingly cooperate in a combined German-Dutch corps in NATO. They remember, above all, those who fought and died to liberate them, those men of the First Canadian Army who came from afar to drive the Germans out of Holland, those RCAF pilots who supported the armies and dropped food to them in the hungry days just before liberation, and the RCN sailors who cleared mines and ferried supplies.

Their acts of remembrance were visible in the Canadian war cemeteries at Groesbeek and Holten, both of which are supremely beautiful places, if one can say such a thing of graveyards where thousands of countrymen are buried so far from home. At Holten, several days before V-E Day, there were perhaps a hundred ordinary Dutch families wandering among the endless rows of headstones that—beneath a carved maple leaf—list the rank, name, dates of birth and death, regiment or corps, and sometimes a message from parents, wives, or children. Small children looked solemn as their parents talked to them: these men, these boys—and so many of them were boys who had the demographic bad luck to be born in the 1920s and to grow up knowing little else but the Depression and war—had died to free their nation from oppression. Do not forget what they did for your country. Remember that you are free because of them.

Those Canadians who assume that the liberation of Holland was a cakewalk against a beaten Wehrmacht would be disabused of that notion by the thousands who are buried in these war cemeteries. At Holten, for example, there are twenty men of the Cape Breton Highlanders whose headstones reveal they were killed in action on May 1, 1945, in liberating the little port of Delfzijl, a battle that their regimental history calls its hardest fight of the war. On May 1—with Hitler already a suicide and the war inexorably drawing to its close! The Dutch families at Holten that day understood what their liberation had cost.

The same public display of memory was evident for all to see—including a huge CBC television audience—in the amazing victory parade of Canadians through Apeldoorn, a few days before the V-E Day anniversary. Apeldoorn is a pleasant town of about 100,000 people in central Holland, quiet, staid in the reserved Dutch way. But that day, just as fifty years before when the Canadian Shermans rolled into their towns, the Dutch were far from staid. In May 1995 Apeldoorn's streets were lined by at least a half-million men and women, children, and babes in arms. The 15,000 or so Canadian vets who marched through the streets were mobbed, showered with kisses, handed drinks, smokes, and flags in a sincere outpouring of love, affection, and gratitude. The parade, scheduled to run for about two hours, lasted for eight, so slow was the triumphal progress through the happy crowds. That the vets lasted so long was a tribute to the power of exhilaration to overcome the aches and pains inherent in seventy-five-year-old bodies.

I will never forget the sight of young mothers in their twenties, weeping and cheering simultaneously while holding their babies up to get a sobbing veteran's kiss. The Dutch mothers told astonished Canadian reporters they were doing this so their children could say they had been touched by one of the men who liberated the Netherlands a half-century before.

The Dutch remember. They teach their children about the war in their schools; they teach that freedom is everything and that, if not defended, it can be lost. They take whole schools to the Canadian cemeteries each year to lay flowers on the graves and to make the point that the preservation of freedom has a price.

114

How different it is in Canada today. The Second World War was a time of supreme national effort for Canadians, who produced a military, industrial, and agricultural contribution to victory that was frankly astonishing. Ten percent of the population was in uniform; Canadian war production, starting from effectively nothing, became large enough for us to give to our Allies billions of dollars' worth of weapons and foodstuffs—on a proportionate scale a greater amount than that of the United States. There was scarcely a family in the land that did not have someone in the service, either as a volunteer, as were the vast majority, or as a conscript. There is no doubt, however, that the war was fought in large measure by Canadians of British origin.

This fact may partly explain the curious way we study—or do not study—the war in our schools. In this new multicultural Canada, the history of the world wars is seen as a divisive force, something that is almost too dangerous to teach in primary and secondary schools. What might a child of German or Slovakian or Croatian origin think, how might the youngster feel, if the Second World War was discussed in any detail? Better to say nothing, or look at the war only in terms of its impact on female workers in munitions plants, or stress the unjust way Canada treated Japanese Canadians or barred Jewish refugees fleeing from Hitler. The pride that Canadians should feel in their substantial role in the war, the lessons its events should hold for us, are brushed aside by the efforts to create a history that suits the misguided ideas of contemporary Canada held by successive federal and provincial governments and by far too many academics.

"Freedom's just another word for nothing left to lose," as a once-popular song put it, and certainly that is how Canadian schools and universities treat it in their avoidance of our war history. But the song is dead wrong: freedom is the word for what is most precious, for what cannot be lost, a word and a concept for which so many Canadians fought and too many died. The children and grandchildren of the Dutch who lived through the war and brutal occupation understand this and remember what can happen if freedom is lost; pathetically, terribly, the children and grandchildren of those who liberated them do not.

The veterans still remember. They have become inured to public indifference, to sincere, well-meaning, but largely unattended ceremonies on Remembrance Day, and to the small crowds that celebrated the events of a half-century ago. Still, the celebrations of the milestones of the war—the fiftieth anniversary commemorations of the Battle of Britain, the Battle of the Atlantic, the D-Day invasion, and V-E Day (the Italian campaign was largely neglected, just as it was during the war!)—were critically important to the vets. All now old men and women with their memories becoming ever more important, the fiftieth anniversaries were their collective swan song. How fortunate that the Dutch knew how to sing their praises, even if most Canadians did not.

It was not only Canadians in general who failed to remember or sing the vets' praises; it was also the Canadian Broadcasting Corporation and the National Film Board, two agencies of the government of Canada that in January 1992 combined to show on national television *The Valour and the Horror*, a three-part series that looked at the Second World War. Prepared by Brian and Terence McKenna, experienced film and television journalists, *The Valour and the Horror* was a self-conscious attempt to look at the war from a new slant, one that tried to be "fair" to the Nazis. For the McKennas, everything was relative, even a world war that was fought to save freedom and democracy. In their view, generals and officers strove for personal glory as they threw away their troops at Hong Kong and in futile attacks in Normandy. British air marshals ordered gullible Canadian bomber crews to destroy German cities and civilians, and in defending the Reich it was the German night-fighter pilots, not the Allies, who had the moral high ground. All three parts in the series were a perversion of reality, a misreading of history through lenses tinted pink in the aftermath of Vietnam antiwar-era sentimentality. All wars are equally evil and no war can be just, the McKennas apparently believed; the poor bloody infantry, the simple sailor, and the naive airman were inevitably pawns, dupes used for the advantage of cynical statesmen and generals.

"Death by Moonlight," the part on the Canadians' role in the Bomber Command offensive, barely conveyed that the Nazis had started the war and had begun bombing cities. The blitz on London and Coventry was not part of their lexicon. Nor was there much understanding of the power and efficiency of the German army, which made attack across the English Channel such a risky enterprise and all but compelled Britain to use its only weapon, Bomber Command, against Germany. The weaknesses of radar, the difficulties of finding precise targets in darkness deepened by

117

blackouts, the limits of aircraft technology all made cities the only possible targets for the Wellington, Halifax, and Lancaster bombers. Massive bomber raids against Germany were the only way of destroying the morale and the industrial sites of an enemy of unprecedented dangerousness. What other methods could have been employed? Could victory have been won without using the maximum available force against Germany? Without the proper historical context, it was easy for the McKennas to portray the air offensive against Germany as genocidal in intent.

The reaction to *The Valour and the Horror* from former servicemen—all of whom understood instinctively the power that television had to shape the way their grandchildren viewed the world—was shock, hurt, and outrage. They had watched their friends overcome their fear to fly against powerful defences, they had seen thousands die, and now they were being painted by their own countrymen and the national broadcasting network as baby-killers. Not only had the McKennas suggested a moral equivalence between the Nazis and the RCAF, but they had failed to understand or recognize that the Allies were fighting to preserve the civilization Hitler was trying to destroy. The films suggested that their cause, their sacrifices, were every bit as detestable as were the Nazis; their victory was for naught, and good and evil had somehow become one. "I couldn't believe my ears that they would show something like that," said Donald Elliott, an RCAF bomber crew member who had been shot down over Germany in 1941. "By telling untruths and innuendo, everything in the film—the music, the words, the way that people were depicted—all of it implied that we were either war criminals, knowing what we were doing, or that we were dupes that just followed orders and just dumped our bombs on German cities without caring where they went. And if they killed women and children, well, tough luck."

The result for the veterans was a long, losing campaign against the McKennas and their films. The Senate Subcommittee on Veterans Affairs held hearings in 1992 that turned into a war between those who sought historical accuracy and those who supported free speech. The McKennas argued that there were no errors in their programs, that their version of truth was seamless. The senators, however, decided that "Death by Moonlight" was a "filmed editorial," and it recommended that the CBC not rebroadcast the series in its original form. The CBC ombudsman conducted an investigation and declared the programs "flawed," failing to measure up to the CBC's standards. But when the Canadian Radio-television and Telecommunications Commission got into the act, its judgment contrarily supported the programs' accuracy and balance. Then it was to the courts, when veterans, claiming defamation, launched a class-action suit against the McKennas, the CBC, and the National Film Board. That case dragged on until 1995, when the suit was tossed out by the Ontario Court of Appeal.

So the surviving aircrew lost. But did the McKennas win? In the eyes of journalists, who rallied behind their brethren, probably so:

freedom of speech had been preserved in the face of an attack by those who wanted their particular view of events to prevail. But in the eyes of the public, the McKennas had been badly battered, and thousands who had never heard of the bomber offensive (or even the Second World War) had the opportunity to learn what their grandfathers had done fifty years before, the chance to see old men girding their loins to fight once more for what they believe in. Most important, perhaps, *The Valour and the Horror* seemed unlikely to make it into classrooms for use during Remembrance Day observances. Unfortunately, when a group of veterans raised the money to produce *No Price Too High*, a balanced portrayal of the nation at war, the CBC refused to televise it. It was left to cable channels and, eventually, PBS in the United States to tell the veterans' story. What clearly emerges from this unhappy tale is that the memory of the Second World War is all but gone from our society. With the exception of the ever-dwindling band of veterans, the war is only a dim memory.

120 Why are we so ignorant? The lamentable failure of our schools in treating the wars—and all of Canadian history—is a large part of it. This neglect begins in the universities, for it is the university history departments that train most of the history teachers for primary and secondary classrooms. Let me begin by considering the account of the two world wars in

the *History of the Canadian Peoples*, the best-selling text already referred to in Chapter 3. The account of the Great War focuses on the conscription election of 1917; the actual fighting receives only six short paragraphs and a half-page sidebar. The account of trench warfare is essentially correct, though the number of casualties, and especially those wounded in action, is misstated. The most extraordinary aspect of the few words on the war is in the sidebar "'Manpower' and the War." The military's "exclusionary" policies are denounced for increasing the shortage of soldiers for the front: "Despite the eagerness of some women to serve overseas," we are told, "they were unwelcome on the front lines." Women were permitted to serve only as nurses, and forty-seven died, "victims of enemy attack and disease contracted from patients." When non-white males volunteered, "they, too, were often turned away" because they might "offend the racist sensibilities of the men at the front." Some of this is correct, but to suggest that Canada could have welcomed female soldiers for front-line service is simply bizarre. The attitudes and culture of 1917 Canada simply would not have permitted it; no government on either side of the war allowed women to fight as combatants. How the textbook's authors could not know this, how they would write as they did, is unclear—unless they were determined to emphasize the anti-female attitudes of a male, white government even to the point of grossly misrepresenting history.

121

When the *History of the Canadian Peoples* turns to the Second World War, we begin with a capsule treatment of the conscription issue that is unexceptional. Then we are told that while Prime Minister King resisted pressures in favour of conscription, "he was unwilling to reduce Canada's commitment to the Allied war effort," a phrasing that suggests he should have done so. This "failure" appears to be responsible for the decision in November 1944 to send home-defence conscripts overseas, a decision that provoked mutinies in camps in British Columbia. Nothing is said to suggest that the lack of infantry reinforcements was leading to higher casualties among units fighting in Italy and Northwest Europe. The implication is that a capricious government, neglecting the impressive French-Canadian contribution to the war, acted unthinkingly and, as a result, "strengthened the credibility of Quebec nationalists and added to feelings of betrayal among French Canadians." That the soldiers overseas might have felt betrayed if they were not reinforced never enters the authors' minds.

The text then gives incorrect numbers on enlistment in the three services, and in one brief paragraph treats the war fronts on which Canadians served. "In December 1941, Canadian forces were involved in a futile attempt to dislodge the Japanese from the British colony of Hong Kong," a wording that implies that the Canadians were invading rather than defending the island. The Dieppe fiasco is mentioned, with casualty figures, closing with a bald statement that ends the paragraph:

"Canadians also participated in the liberation of Europe, including the invasions of Sicily in 1943 and Normandy in 1944." So much for the efforts of the First Canadian Army, the RCAF, and the Royal Canadian Navy.

We then get a longer paragraph than the preceding one on women's role in the armed forces ("Although only men participated in combat, 43,000 [the correct number is more than 50,000] women in uniform worked behind the lines"), and a longer one still on wartime civil rights abuses in Canada. German and Italian Canadians were "imprisoned without trial . . . on the basis of flimsy evidence connecting them to the Nazis or fascists," we are told. That there were active Nazi and Italian Fascist groups in Canada and that they had been spreading propaganda and raising money for their masters in Berlin and Rome does not make it into the story; rather, the impression is deliberately established that the government again was acting capriciously and brutally. The Japanese-Canadian story is told somewhat more fairly, as the authors at least recognize, as some other texts do not, that the Japanese Canadians were evacuated from the west coast, not interned, and that some Japanese Canadians might have been disloyal.

123

What impression might a university student take away from these accounts of the world wars? Canada's governments were overcommitted to the fighting; they acted brutally toward and discriminated against women, ethnic Canadians, and racial minorities, and trampled underfoot the rights of

French Canadians; and the contribution to the fighting by Canadians in the Second World War was insignificant except for the Hong Kong and Dieppe defeats. To say that such accounts view the war through a distorted lens is surely an understatement. What makes this distortion all the more extraordinary is that the two world wars were genuine "people's wars" for Canadians, calling forth extraordinary efforts from men and women both overseas and at home. No other events of the twentieth century had a greater impact on Canada, but the authors of the *History of the Canadian Peoples* are so intent on painting a tale of prejudice, bias, maltreatment, and discrimination that they almost completely omit the people they claim to be chronicling.

Other university texts are surprisingly similar in approach. They will have a page or sometimes only a paragraph on the fighting at the front in each war, but invariably the emphasis is on the troubles of the home front. University history "readers" that collect articles for classroom discussion and are designed to accompany textbooks almost never have any coverage of fighting overseas, most of the space being devoted to the mistreatment of minorities or women's role in factories. It is, as more than one writer has noted, part of a concerted effort to create a Canada out of ideological fantasy—a Canada dedicated to caring, neutrality, and peacekeeping.

The attitude that underlies the mistreatment of the history of the wars derives from a reaction against "certain assumptions about human nature which excuse or justify competition and aggression." Queen's University's Katherine McKenna (no relative of *The Valour and the Horror* McKennas, but their ideological soulmate) wrote in 1989 of being baffled "by the almost universal viewpoint my students have expressed about the naturalness of conflict between people. War, they have told me, is inevitable. Peace is idealistic, utopian and unnatural." Why should students feel this way? Because, she continues, in most school courses "the traditional emphasis on wars and political conflict as the driving forces of history remains intact"—something I might suggest is no longer even remotely true. If only women had shaped history— "their activities," McKenna said, "for the most part have historically been more nurturant and co-operative." Cooperation and peace should be taught, McKenna goes on, although these are the attitudes students see as weak and unrealistic because they have been "taught a biased view of history and human nature." This condemnatory approach to the way history has been written (and the way history has been made!) has certainly captured most present-day textbook writers, male and female, and it probably explains why the fighting has been all but eliminated from the Canadian history of the world wars.

It also explains why peacekeeping, a useful modern specialty of Canada's armed forces, has been elevated into a principle. Peacekeeping is the traditional Canadian military activity, we are told on television, in the press, before parliamentary committees, and increasingly in the textbooks used in schools. The sole national military monument erected since the Second World War commemorates the efforts and sacrifices of Canadian peacekeepers—and so it should. But peacekeeping, however helpful it may be (and there is substantial doubt about its effectiveness in Cyprus, the Middle East, Somalia, and elsewhere), can only be one small part of this country's military role. Professor McKenna undoubtedly admires peacekeeping because it counters the ideas of male aggressiveness she rightly abhors. But the peacekeepers are necessary because so much of the world *is* aggressive, because men *and* women, inflamed by nationalist or racialist passions, slaughter each other with abandon. Wishing for peace doesn't create it; teaching that peace is the norm—and omitting to teach the history of the wars—doesn't bring peace any closer.

One reader of the politically correct history texts used in Canadian universities, Robert Martin of the law faculty of the University of Western Ontario, wrote in the *Globe and Mail* on November 11, 1991, that he had lost his father in action in the Falaise Gap in August 1944, and, when he read several recent texts in Canadian history, he discovered that "the Second World War has disappeared. The years between 1939 and 1945 are still there, but the war is gone. My father and thousands of other Canadians have been airbrushed out of history." Martin noted that the texts and readers offer nothing of what the war was about or what it meant to Canadians, nothing on Nazism, Italian Fascism, or Japanese militarism. Instead, there were articles and

126

accounts of women in the workforce or the evacuation of Japanese Canadians. "I am astounded," Martin said, "that professional historians purport to assess the social effects of a war without ever alluding to why the war was being fought." He added that he lost his father the first time at Falaise and the second time in Canadian history texts. His article provoked a flood of supportive mail and substantial outrage among veterans who believed, rightly enough, that their history was being forgotten when it was not misrepresented again. This biased treatment of the wars in widely used texts and readers explains much about what university graduates know and don't know.

With the example set by the writers of university textbooks, it is no surprise that their former students now teaching in the public and high schools emulate their professors. J.B. Cruxton and W.D. Wilson's *Spotlight Canada* is unusual in devoting substantial space to the international context, to the history of the world wars, and to the efforts and sacrifices of those in the Canadian Armed Forces. But, predictably, it has a full chapter on the Japanese Canadians, a chapter claiming that all of them were interned.

I suppose some learning is better than none at all. A vice-principal from Surrey, British Columbia, asked in the *Globe and Mail* on November 9, 1996, why, on Remembrance Day in her school, she should have "some veteran from the legionnaires come in and stand up there and bore us all to death with his medals"? This attitude is widespread and becoming more so.

Fortunately, there are still teachers in British Columbia who try very hard to ensure that their students learn about Canada's military past. The war years are an integral part of the grade 11 social studies curriculum, military history is covered as thoroughly as is the home front, and, in May 1995, Armstrong's Pleasant Valley Secondary School held an open house on the theme of the Second World War. The school also goes on a field trip to Europe each year and makes a point of visiting the battle-fields. As teacher Dick Lonsdale noted, "Our V.E. Day +50 was something to behold—old men looking at projects with students, eyes brimming with tears and locating where they had been in Holland or Italy." Good teachers with a sense of the past can still make a difference, whatever provincial ministries may try to make them teach.

Meanwhile, in Nova Scotia, as the fiftieth anniversary of V-E Day was marked overseas, the Department of Education sent out nothing to teachers on Canada's part in the Second World War. "Ironically," wrote one teacher to the *Globe and Mail*, "at the very moment that V-E Day was forgotten . . . my school board held a full-day in-service [training session] for teachers on human rights. Nobody noticed that we wouldn't have been there celebrating our tolerance and diversity if more than a million Canadians hadn't joined in the fight against the greatest threat to human rights the modern world has known." No one, she added sadly, "bothered to take a day, an hour—even a minute—to thank them."

In most schools on Remembrance Day there is still an assembly with the ritual reciting of John McCrae's "In Flanders Fields," but what is presented cannot be guaranteed to have any significance. Some schools try hard, however. At Lawrence Park Collegiate in Toronto, pictures of students from the school who were killed during the wars are shown, along with a recitation of where they served and were killed in action, and how old they were when they died. Other schools put on plays focusing on an individual from the school who served. At many institutions, however, the provincial guidelines and the boards of education try to juggle Remembrance Day into relevance with the focus on a war (the Gulf War?) students might remember more clearly than the Great War, and with the ever-present de-emphasis on Canada. Teachers at one high school in Toronto told me they had been discouraged from trying to make their November 11 ceremony "more Canadian." It never seems to occur to administrators that the Lawrence Park approach not only respects Canadian history and those who served but, simultaneously, sends a powerful anti-war message.

Somehow, without Canadians really noticing it, the debt owed to those who fought and died to secure our future has been swept aside. The sense grows that once the vets have all finally died and their embarrassing presence is no more, Remembrance Day observances will be allowed to lapse. Certainly, attempts in 1996 to get a special curriculum for November 11 into the Ontario schools were stonewalled in the

Ministry of Education, notwithstanding a Progressive Conservative government that had claimed to be interested in getting history back into the schools. Too old, too boring, too much violence seemed to be the rationale.

The result of this neglect is obvious in every schoolroom, as Dan Gardner, a teacher volunteer in a Toronto high school in 1995, discovered. Even though they had had the grade 9 or 10 course on Canadian history, his grade 13 students in an optional Canadian course did not know who Winston Churchill was, who the combatants were, or why Canada was involved in the Second World War. To Gardner, this ignorance was incredible. "The war is not just another subject," he wrote in the *Globe and Mail*. "It is a metaphor for what Canada aspires to be. . . The Canadian struggle in the Second World War is as important to Canada as the American Revolution is to the United States. That war, more than any other event, created the modern Canada," he went on. "The war was the fight of freedom and liberal democracy against demonstrable evils. It was the just war. Canada was the little guy rising in surprising strength to defend human dignity. It is a magnificent metaphor for a splendid ideal."

130

But let us be honest. When the two world wars are considered, some of this ignorance is completely understandable. It is more than eight decades since the Battle of Vimy Ridge in 1917, more than fifty years since the end of the Second World War; whole generations have grown up, raised children, and neared retirement since Hong Kong, Dieppe, the Falaise Gap, and Hiroshima and Nagasaki. The travails of the past, whatever their importance to grandparents and to historians, are inevitably less significant for a seventeen year old than a date on Saturday night or the bleak prospects of summertime employment.

Still, the world wars and Canada's role in them are important, too important to be forgotten or to go untaught in the schools. In the Great War, Canada was a colony that had neither a role nor a voice in the decision to begin hostilities. All that Canada could do was to decide how it would participate. In the climate of 1914, in the even more heated atmosphere of 1917, decisions were made that shaped the domestic political context for the rest of the century—and possibly beyond. English Canadians wanted to support Britain to the maximum extent possible, even if that required conscripting those who would not volunteer for overseas service. French-speaking Canadians, farmers, and recent immigrants did not see how Canadian interests, their interests, were directly involved in a struggle between rival empires. The ensuing conscription crisis persuaded French Canadians that English Canadians owed their primary loyalty elsewhere and, moreover, that they would stop at nothing to get their way. Ballot rigging, gerrymandering, corruption—all could be and were justified by the necessity of winning the war. Quebec did not forget.

As important, the Great War made Canadians conscious that they were a nation. Half the men who served in the Canadian Expeditionary Force in the First World War were British-born.

But the Canadian Corps established such a reputation for ferocity in attack that the immigrant colonials found themselves transformed into Canadians. Many veterans recalled attacking at Vimy Ridge in April 1917 as soldiers of the empire, but waking up the day after their great victory as Canadians, full of pride at their maple leaf badges. The war mattered to Canadians, and it gave them a sense of nationhood that has helped to define this country ever since.

In the Second World War, the depressing domestic political history of the Great War repeated itself. Canada again went to war because Britain did, though this time Canada's Parliament made its own decision on entry. Quebec was unhappy, but it went along because Prime Minister King had pledged that there would be no conscription for overseas service. Those promises began to be watered down as soon as the war turned against the Allies. First it was home-defence conscription for thirty days, then ninety days, then the duration of the war. Next it was a plebiscite asking all Canada to release the government from its no-conscription pledge to Quebec. In the autumn of 1944, home-defence conscripts were shipped overseas to provide reinforcements for the hard-pressed Canadian divisions fighting in Italy and Northwest Europe. Again, Quebec's sense of betrayal was huge.

These events, whose consequences we still live with, were important, but so too was the more positive impact of the wars. The efforts of the Canadian soldiers in Sicily, Italy, France, Belgium, and the Netherlands in the Second World War were prodigious, and the roles of the Royal Canadian Navy in the Battle of the Atlantic and of the Royal Canadian Air Force in the air war were impressive in achievement and numbers. Moreover, the struggles overseas largely industrialized Canada, creating factories across the land. Agricultural and mineral development was similarly spurred. At the same time, the wars brought women in their tens of thousands into the workplace, taking them away from farms, small towns, and service as parlour maids to a different life and the possibility of earning a living wage. The emancipation of women, not to mention the right to vote, came out of war. And, above all, the idea that Canada was a small, unimportant colony could scarcely be sustained when the Canadian Corps was the premier formation on the Western front, when the First Canadian Army, the Royal Canadian Air Force, and the Royal Canadian Navy were important players in the war against the unspeakable evil of the Nazis. Canada was not a great power, but it was the most important of the middle powers, a nation deserving a place at the table when questions of war and peace were discussed.

Historian Patrick Brennan wrote recently in the *Calgary Herald*: "Few Canadians of my generation, the 'baby boomers,' or those even younger, have ever heard of Vimy Ridge, let alone its deep significance in our country's history. Sometimes," he wrote, "I meet students who have visited the now pastoral site, surrounded by meticulously kept cemeteries, on their summer explorations of Europe. They all seem moved by the experience,

133

this surprise discovery of a powerful emotional link to their collective past." Of course, the students are moved, but it ought not be a surprise. Vimy Ridge, Passchendaele, the Hundred Days, Dieppe, Hong Kong, Ortona, the Falaise Gap, the clearing of the Scheldt, the liberation of the Netherlands, the Atlantic convoy war, and the air war over Britain and Germany should be part of the collective consciousness of all Canadians, young and old, native-born and recently arrived. The wars are part of Canada's heritage, a proud part.

To remember the causes and events of the wars is to realize the evil that men can do and the enormous courage with which ordinary men and women can face unimaginable horror and overcome fear for a good cause. To remember Vimy, for example, is to recall the cold, misty Easter morning, the thousands of soldiers of the four Canadian divisions fighting together for the first time, moving out of their trenches against German lines that had resisted earlier French and British attacks. So perfect were the plans, so determined and well-prepared the attackers, that the ridge was taken in a great victory. The ten thousand casualties suffered in that victory ensured that no one could feel much glory, but the pride in achievement was real. So it deserved to be. At Vimy, Brennan said, Canada—English Canada, at least—came of age under heart-rending circumstances. The great war monument there, the largest erected by any of the belligerents, expressed Canada's pride and sorrow, two of the components of the nation's collective memory.

The Flanders fields in which Canadians fought during the Great War and again in the Second World War are peaceful now, though farmers still turn up skeletons and occasional rusted shells. The wars live in the memory of Europeans much more than in our newer society, and that is appropriate enough. But Canadians should not, cannot, forget their forefathers' efforts. Too much of our history was made there, too much of our blood spilled. The struggles that the Canadian Corps and the First Canadian Army went through laid the foundation for the Canada we have today. Rich, prosperous, still struggling for unity, present-day Canada was made in Flanders fields. We dare not forget. After the commemorations of D-Day and V-E Day, I know that I cannot.

CHAPTER 6

Resurrecting Canadian History

"Nobody wants to talk about Canada," Brian Moore has one of the characters in his early novel *The Luck of Ginger Coffey* say. "Canada is a bore." I might paraphrase this comment only slightly to say that "no one wants to talk about Canada's national history. It's a bore."

We certainly treat it that way. Yet no history that involves massive immigration across fierce seas in small boats or cramped ocean liners; that recounts wresting a half-continent from the wilderness, settling it, and constructing great cities and small towns; that includes wars at home and abroad, and the struggles for dignity and success of countless ordinary men, women, and children can be boring. But somehow, for all the reasons laid out in this book, we have all but killed Canadian history.

Who, in particular, is responsible for this decimation of our history?

- The provincial ministries of education for preaching and practising parochial regionalism and for gutting their curricula of content.
- The ministry bureaucrats who have pressed the "whole child" approach and anti-élitist education.
- The ethnic communities that have been conned by Canada's multiculturalism policy into demanding an offence-free education for all Canadian children, so that the idea that Canada has a past and a culture has been all but lost.
- The boards of education that have responded to pressures for political correctness by denuding their curricula of serious knowledge and offering only trendy pap.
- The media that has looked only for scandal and for a new approach to the past, so that fact becomes half truth and feeds only cynicism.
- The university professors who have waged internecine wars to such an extent that they have virtually destroyed history, and especially Canadian history, as a serious discipline.
- The university presses and the agencies that subsidize professors for publishing unreadable books on miniscule subjects.
- The federal governments that have been afraid to reach over provincial governments and the school boards to give Canadians what they want and need: a sense that they live in a nation with a glorious past and a great future.

Our history is dead or perhaps on life support. Can it be restored to life?

The basic task falls to parents, who must tell their teachers and principals, their school trustees and school boards, and their provincial governments that they want their children to learn the history of their country. They must demand that Canadian history be set properly in the context of the West and of the world, where it belongs. They must insist that it be Canadian history, not history filtered through a provincial or a regional lens or given a multicultural tilt. By all means, Nova Scotia and Alberta should teach about their histories and their regions, but they must teach about Canada's past, too. Of course, native history should be studied, just as that of the immigrants who made Canada what it is. But the history of the nation must be learnt as well. There should be a minimum of three years of compulsory history in the public schools, and a further three courses in high school. And these courses must be grounded solidly in chronology, and must treat both the political *and* the social history of the nation. They must teach students how the nation and the world work, how our civilization developed, and why it values the concepts that it does.

Parents should also support every attempt to raise standards, to have their children pushed to the maximum in class. Every effort at testing literacy, every attempt to establish provincial and national standards in history and every other subject should be enthusiastically welcomed. Canadian schools at every level from kindergarten to university, despite what we tell ourselves,

141

can and must be better. We deserve this. We pay vast sums for education, and we are simply not getting the returns we should.

The nation needs clear, measurable standards for history. The United States' effort to secure such standards failed despite the best efforts of educators, but that is no reason for Canadians not to try. Simply talking about standards would increase interest and focus attention. First, the federal government might consider establishing a Centre for Canadian History and locating it near, but not at, a major university. The centre should have the task of drawing up history standards for the public and high schools, testing them in selected classrooms, and commissioning the writing of textbooks for public and high schools that reflect these standards. Once the ground has been thoroughly prepared, the prime minister could call a conference of the Council of Ministers of Education to sell these standards to the provinces. The goal should be a common curriculum of compulsory history courses in the public schools and high schools—with added provincial wrinkles. Of course, Quebec nationalists will scream, British Columbia's premier will posture, and Ontario's education minister will look hurt when his own government's paltry efforts at teaching history are compared with what they could and should be. But perhaps the effort might change the way the past is presented to Canadian students. At the very least, such an effort would demonstrate that Ottawa thinks the Canadian past is important, a force for unity in a country that desperately needs to strengthen the bonds that tie it together. Our common past is one such bond.

The federal government could use the same meeting of ministers to announce the creation of a scheme of Canadian Scholarships, lightly modelled on the National Merit Scholarships in the United States or, even better, on the *Studienstiftung des Deutschen Volkes*. Early on in the grade 11 year, all the students who wished to participate could pay a small fee to write examinations in various subject areas, most definitely including Canadian history. These examinations would be marked by a national panel of teachers and professors. The best students, no more than 500 each year, would receive the designation of Canadian Scholar and, say, $2500 for each year of university in which they maintain an A average. The cash is important, but the Canadian Scholar designation, if the scheme is rigorously selective, will be worth even more at university admission time, and in prestige. For Ottawa to say that intelligence and hard work matter, that brains constitute a healthy élitism, would be a tonic for every educator—and for students who have been raised to believe that having brains defines one as a nerd.

In its Speech from the Throne and its leader's day address on September 23 and 24, 1997, the Chrétien government announced as a millennium project a huge endowment fund to finance university scholarships for low- and middle-income students. The details remain undetermined, but merit apparently is to be a requirement, not just economic status, and this is a major step forward for which the government deserves plaudits.

There is much more to be done. Ottawa could announce its

intention to use this Centre for Canadian History to direct a scheme to feed the best students in our high schools a richer diet than they now receive. Every high school that wishes to do so could teach its best students history, literature, mathematics, and science at a first-year university level, and have those students sit a national test in each of the subjects studied. In history, such tests must contain a substantial piece of writing, and the examinations again should be centrally marked. Such courses should ordinarily be taught in the last year of high school, and the grades could be given on the normal A to F system. The universities should be pushed and cajoled into giving a student with an A grade two one-semester credits. A first-rate student, sitting three or four tests, could enter university with most of the first year already done, and this plan would permit either an accelerated university degree or extra flexibility in taking or delaying courses. Above all, such a scheme would again encourage the best students and the best high school teachers. The costs might be substantial, but Ottawa could carry them as a useful federal intrusion into the educational field.

Ottawa could also take other useful measures, such as offering public schools and high schools grants to purchase books in Canadian history for their libraries. The government could give subscriptions to the few readable journals about Canadian history to every high school library in the nation—*The Beaver*, say, and *National History*. It could fund a Canadian history Web site on the Internet and begin to speed up the process of putting national archival records on-line. It could set up a clearinghouse, possibly located at the Centre for Canadian History, for the distribution of Canadian history materials. And it could have the Canadian Heritage ministry offer additional financial support for television and radio history programs. A first-rate television series set around Canada's national parks or national historic sites, for example, would be a natural.

The federal government could also emulate two other useful foreign innovations. For more than two decades, American foundations, businesses, and trade unions have supported local, state, and national competitions for students in public schools and high schools under the rubric of National History Day. Each year, tens of thousands of children produce historical videos, interview veterans or workers, gather documents, and write essays on a broad historical topic. The results are increasingly sophisticated, the interest generated is huge, and there are prizes that inspire students and teachers to discover their local, regional, and national past. Why should we not have a similar plan here, one that brings together students in French and English from every province and territory? The costs are relatively small—my estimate is about $400,000 a year—and the benefits in student involvement and in creating an appreciation of the nation's past could be very substantial indeed. In France, moreover, on a September weekend, the government opens more than 10,000 monuments and public and private museums free of charge, schedules and coordinates thousands of events—from open houses to talks to participatory recreations—all devoted to the nation's rich past; and publishes a book-size program setting out what's on and where. This history and heritage festival is hugely successful for adults and children. Such a Canadian event could dovetail neatly with Canadian History Day, as a Canadian school program might well be called.

Yet another federal effort might be to establish five chairs in national history in Canadian universities. The government funds multicultural history chairs, and it has established chairs in strategic studies across the country, many of which encompass military history. Why should it not put up money for the study of Canada's national history, defined as political and diplomatic history? Some of the social historians might object, as they did to the establishment of strategic studies chairs, but so what? It is always going to be hard to move universities and departments that are proud of their autonomy. National history chairs would be an intrusion, yes, but one solidly based on precedent, and their creation might help speed the movement toward the study of national history that is already under way in universities abroad.

These ideas cost money. They involve difficult political and academic choices, and they would undoubtedly involve Ottawa in battles with the provinces. But our governments are elected to serve us, and sometimes they don't do their jobs very well. To have provincial governments that actually pushed their students to learn and to achieve in school would be a proper use of public funds. To have a national government that acted as if it actually represented a nation would be a change that is long overdue. Happily, there is a sign that Prime Minister Chrétien may wish to move precisely in this direction. In his September 24, 1997, speech in Parliament, he indicated his concern with the results of the Dominion Institute's survey. "It is unacceptable," he said, "that our youth may know all about computers, but so little about their country." Then, in a key paragraph, he added:

> We must find ways for young Canadians to learn what they share, to know what we have done, and to gain pride in their nation's accomplishments. The Government of Canada will work with our great museums, other federal and provincial institutions and with voluntary groups to develop ways to increase Canadians' knowledge of what we have done together.

If the government follows through, as I believe it will, this leadership could result in programs that could save our history.

Canadians are the world's most fortunate of peoples. We live at a North American standard of living and yet have few of the burdens and difficulties that beset the superpower to our south. We have a past of selfless service to freedom and democracy; we are all but free of atrocities; and our national sins, weighed in the global balance, are minor. We have much to celebrate, and much in our past, present, and future to admire. Yet we beat our

147

collective breasts, moan about our imagined historical transgressions, and haggle endlessly about the division of the spoils between federal and provincial governments. Perhaps if we studied our past, we could find the inspiration to deal with our current problems. There is nothing today comparable to the crises that faced Upper and Lower Canadians when the Americans were poised to invade in 1812; nothing to compare with the difficulties that beset the Fathers of Confederation as they tried to shape the dominion during and after the American Civil War; nothing that can compare with the great racial splits that transfixed the nation's attention during the conscription crises of the world wars; and, happily, nothing that can compare with the economic deprivation that beset millions during the Great Depression. If only we knew our past, we might appreciate the relative simplicity of the national tensions that face us.

History is no panacea for our national ailments. But a nation cannot forget its past, obliterate it, subdivide it into micro-histories, alter it, and bury it. Too often in the last half-century, Canadians seem to have done just that, and it is time to restore the past to its proper place in our national cultural consciousness, in our schools and universities, and in our public discourse.

148

If Canada is to be worthy of its envied standing in the world, if it is to offer something to its own people and to humanity, it will have to forge a national spirit that can unite its increasingly diverse peoples. We cannot achieve this unanimity unless we teach our national history, celebrate our founders, establish new symbols, and strengthen the terms of our citizenship. We will never be able to achieve it if we continue to allow the educational theorists and the timid provincial politicians to control the agenda. We have a nation to save and a future to build. How much easier it will be to accomplish these goals if Canadians in every province and region can begin from the firm foundation of our history.

Index

J. L. GRANATSTEIN is one of our most distinguished historians and the author of over 45 books, including *Yankee Go Home?* and *Victory 1945* (with Desmond Morton). *The Generals* won the J.W. Dafoe Prize and the UBC Medal for Canadian Biography. The Royal Society of Canada awarded him the J.B. Tyrrell Historical Gold Medal (1992) for "outstanding work in the history of Canada." In 1996, the Conference of Defence Associations Institute named him winner of the Vimy Award. In 1997 he received the Order of Canada. A Distinguished Research Professor of History Emeritus at York University, he has received honorary degrees from Memorial University and the University of Calgary and is a member of the RMC Board of Governors. He is the Director and Chief Executive Officer of the Canadian War Museum in Ottawa.